the
Jesus
experiment

the
Jesus
experiment

What happens when you follow in his footsteps?

bill perkins

Tyndale House Publishers, Inc.
Carol Stream, Illinois

Library of Congress Cataloging-in-Publication Data

Perkins, Bill, date.
    The Jesus experiment : what happens when you follow in his footsteps? / Bill Perkins.
        p. cm.
    Includes bibliographical references (p.   ).
    ISBN 978-1-4143-1142-5 (sc)
    1. Jesus Christ—Example. I. Title.
    BT304.2.P46 2011
    232.9'04—dc23   2011026600

To Paul Perkins.
You've made me proud.

The Jesus Experiment
[Revised order of study]

Lesson #1 "The Jesus Experiment"
Book: Week 1

Lesson #2 "Abiding in Jesus"
Book: Week 2

Lesson #3 "Jesus Prayed"
Book: Week 3

Lesson #4 "Jesus Overcame Temptation"
Book: Week 5

Lesson #5 "Jesus Had a Mission"
Book: Week 6

Lesson #6 "Jesus Took Action"
Book: Week 7

Lesson #7 "Jesus Did the Unexpected"
Book: Week 8

Lesson #8 "Jesus Offered Hope"
Book: Week 10

Lesson #9 "Jesus Blessed Children"
Book: Week 11

guest? ⟵⟶ **Lesson # 10 "Jesus Loved the Difficult"**
Book: Week 12

March 25 – **Lesson #11 "Jesus Humbly Served**
Book: Week 9

April 1 **Lesson # 12 "Jesus Faced His Fear"**
Book: Week 4

Contents

Introduction

WE'VE ALL HEARD the familiar phrase, "Don't judge a book by its cover." Though there's wisdom in the statement, I don't think it applies to this book. In a very real sense, the cover captures the peril *and* the promise of the Jesus Experiment.

The footprint on water was left by Jesus as he approached the fishing boat Peter and the rest of the disciples were rowing against a raging storm. As Jesus drew near, Peter stepped out of the boat and walked on water. For those windy, wet, and miraculous moments, he, too, left footprints on the Sea of Galilee.

The goal of Christian spirituality is for believers to become more like Christ. I propose that Peter was never more like Jesus than on the night he stepped onto the rolling waves and walked toward him. Of course, the second his eyes left Jesus and he focused on himself and his human limitations, down he went.

In *The Jesus Experiment*, we want to capture the energy and excitement of that first step off the boat. But we don't want to stop there; we don't want to sink. We want to keep moving forward, step-by-step, as we learn *how* to keep our eyes on Jesus and follow him.

Jesus offers his followers "a rich and satisfying life" (John 10:10, NLT). Some translations say "abundant life."

Abundant life sounds great, but what does it actually mean, day-to-day, in the twenty-first century? At the time Jesus made this promise, he was describing himself metaphorically as the good shepherd, the one who protects and provides for his sheep. In ancient Israel, if there was no wooden gate on a sheep pen, the shepherd would lie across the opening at night to sleep. To enter or exit the fold, the sheep had to step over their shepherd. All sheep had to pass through him, like a door, and once they were inside the security of the fold, he provided a good and safe life. That's the picture Jesus offers of himself; it's his self-portrait—he's both the gate and the good shepherd. And only through him, and with him, can we have abundant life.

Think of all the time and effort we spend searching for satisfaction and fulfillment. We look for them in a new house or car, or maybe in a weeklong vacation once a year. We seek them in our jobs, kids, significant others, and education. We strive to achieve them through sports, recreation, and toys. We frantically chase them in sex, music, alcohol, and drugs. We hunt for them in money, status, and power. If we find something that seems to satisfy, it eventually breaks, wears out, falls apart, or becomes boring, like old chewing gum. Or it simply disappears, like spent money, a failed relationship, or a lost job. In a sense, the things or people that promise fulfillment often drain our lives.

Jesus made it clear that "one's life does not consist in the abundance of his possessions" (Luke 12:15, ESV). Yet we continue searching. We're travelers wandering cross-country without a map, pilots flying into a storm without a compass, blind people bumping into other blind people, searching for someone to show us the way. All the while, the "way" has been clearly identified; he is staring us in the face. Jesus said, "You search the Scriptures because you think they give you eternal life. But the Scriptures point to me!" (John 5:39, NLT).

Abundant life isn't a butterfly that will land on your shoulder if you stand still. No, you have to clamber over the gunwales, amid the storms and circumstances of life, and take a step of faith. The good news is that Jesus leads the way. We only have to follow.

When Jesus was on earth, he didn't have a lot of material possessions. At one point, he didn't even have a place to lay his head (Matthew 8:20; Luke 9:58). Yet has anyone ever lived a life more abundantly rich and satisfying? His basic needs were met; he had a real-time, ongoing connection with his Father, living completely in his will; he had a circle of close and trusted friends; his life had purpose and power; and he accomplished everything he set out to accomplish. This is the abundant life Jesus offers his followers, and this is what living the Jesus Experiment will yield.

The purpose of this book is to provide you with a real-time connection with Christ so you can test his promise to give you abundant life.

The purpose of this book is to provide you with a real-time connection with Christ so you can test his promise to give you abundant life.

What is the Jesus Experiment? In a nutshell, it takes the concept of a scientific experiment—to find out if something is true, it must be tested—and applies it to Jesus' claim of abundant life. Maybe this sounds strange to you. You might be asking, how can something spiritual be tested? Yet the Bible teaches that we are to *examine* spiritual claims and "hold fast that which is good" (1 Thessalonians 5:21, NASB). By living the Jesus Experiment, you will examine the validity of Jesus' promise. And, if you're like me, you will soon discover he freely gives the abundant life he promises.

A Spiritual Experiment

I GOT THE idea for the Jesus Experiment several years ago while writing a book based on Jesus' leadership style. After completing the manuscript, I knew I had overlooked something significant. All my research hadn't turned up what I sensed was the most important piece of the puzzle.

And then I asked myself, *In what ways do I want to be like Christ?*

That's when it dawned on me that if I want to be like Jesus, I need to *feel, think, speak,* and *act* like him—as a devoted disciple. It's not that I want to change my personality or become another person. Instead, I want my feelings, thoughts, words, and deeds to be so guided by Jesus that I experience the abundant life he offers.

> *I asked myself,* In what ways do I want to be like Christ?

We see the concept of discipleship in other relationships as well.

For instance, all three of my sons are writers. From their youth, I've coached them and edited their work. Each one is currently writing a book. When they send me pages to read, nothing encourages me more than to see how they've grown as writers. I often recognize myself in their word choices, the cadence of their prose, and their humor—or attempts at humor. I am their teacher, and they are my disciples. As writers, they want to be like me while developing their own voices.

As disciples of Jesus, we want to be like him. We want his life and teaching to shape us so our lives reflect his. We want others to hear in our words and see in our deeds the life of our Teacher and Lord. To facilitate that kind of life, we need something that will enable us to put into practice what we know and are learning about Jesus.

Yet we always face the same shadowy opposing force: *fear.*

Fear

Before I began writing about the Jesus Experiment, it was only an idea; I had nothing to fear because the idea required nothing of me. I could sit around my office, pondering the concepts and stories. But when I decided to write the book, I realized I would first have to *live* the experiment. There would be no room for philosophical musings. I would have to set up the lab, run the test, and evaluate the results in my own life.

What if it didn't work? What if I didn't complete it? What if I failed? What if Jesus' claim failed?

I had never had second thoughts about writing a book. It reminded me of my desire to bungee jump. I've openly told friends, family members, and readers of one of my books that I'd like to leap from a bridge and experience the exhilaration of free-falling fast and far and then feel the bungee cord slow my descent before it launched me up with even greater velocity. Just the thought triggers a mild adrenaline rush. But knowing I want to bungee jump doesn't scare me. Not until a friend actually takes me up on my offer to go bungee jumping and we set a date will I be afraid and have second thoughts.

Part of the reason the Jesus Experiment concerned me is that I knew it would quickly expose how unlike Jesus I am. Though I desire to be more like Christ, my human tendency to remain stuck is strong. Like everyone else, I'm comfortable with the status quo. I have attitudes, habits, and ways of speaking and acting that give me pleasure and calm my nerves—almost like pacifiers—and I don't want to let them go. My fear of rejection and shame prevents me from going into more detail here, and it's this tendency to cover up that reminds me, even as I write these words, that I am still very much *un*like Jesus.

> *Becoming like Christ is a lifelong pursuit . . . and God can accomplish powerful transformation in our lives.*

But that doesn't mean the Jesus Experiment won't work. It only means I have to confront my fears and remind myself of Jesus' promise to give abundant life. If you're feeling similarly apprehensive, I understand; but don't let that hold you back. Let's face it, becoming like Christ is a lifelong pursuit, and something we won't fully attain until he appears and we see him as he is (1 John 3:2). But in the meantime we can be moving in the right direction, and God can accomplish powerful transformation in our lives. It all starts with a simple desire to become more like Jesus and a willingness to *live* the experiment.

A few weeks before I started writing, I knew it was time to give the Jesus Experiment a try. I decided that, for one day, whenever God's Spirit brought it to mind, I would ask myself eight questions:

1. How would Jesus *feel* in this situation?
2. What would Jesus *think* in this situation?

3. What would Jesus *say* in this situation?
4. What would Jesus *do* in this situation?
5. How do *I* feel in this situation?
6. What am *I* thinking in this situation?
7. What am *I* saying in this situation?
8. What am *I* doing in this situation?

At the end of the day, I was encouraged. Seldom had I felt such a real-time connection with Jesus. Throughout the day, as I compared my feelings, thoughts, words, and deeds to his, the differences in our attitudes and actions became clear. Then I asked God to transform me to be more like Christ in my responses.

Here's an example: That afternoon, a driver cut me off on the freeway. My immediate impulse was to camp on the horn—not as a safety warning, but as punishment. But then I asked myself the first four questions. I had to admit Jesus likely wouldn't get annoyed at something so trivial. Nor would he think badly of the offending driver, swear under his breath, or honk his horn. I quickly asked the next four questions and was surprised that the process itself actually settled my spirit. I had made a conscious decision to identify with Jesus and allow him to change me.

Delays and Distractions

I continued the experiment for about a week, until I got distracted. In the back of my mind, I knew I needed to get back on track, but it was always *tomorrow*. And then concern arose as I realized I might not give the experiment a fair shot because of old patterns and habits and the natural force of inertia—an object at rest tends to stay at rest.

It reminded me of a night, many years ago, when my eldest son, Ryan, was a toddler. I was lying on the floor in our home in

Houston, throwing a tennis ball against the wall and catching it. My wife watched me for a moment and then said, "You've got to quit doing that, Bill."

"Why?" I said as I continued to toss the ball against the wall—a bit higher this time.

"Because you've got a son who follows your example, and I don't want him throwing tennis balls in the house."

"But I want to throw it," I said, like a child told to stop playing in the mud.

"Bill, you need to grow up."

That hit a nerve. Something inside told me she was right, but I didn't *want* to grow up. I wanted to keep throwing the ball against the wall. As Cindy stood there, I felt a mixture of certainty and loss. I knew I needed to act like a grown-up and the ball-tossing inside the house would have to stop. I also felt as if a part of me were dying, like I was a boy about to lose an arm—or, if not an arm, at least the freedom to use it to throw balls in the house.

I felt a similar reluctance at the beginning of the Jesus Experiment. Even though I knew it was time to mature in my faith, I was afraid that becoming more like Christ would mean giving up things I enjoyed. Frankly, I wasn't sure I was ready.

If you want to become more like Christ and experience the abundant life he promises, you must change.

Here's the simple truth about the Jesus Experiment: If you want to become more like Christ and experience the abundant life he promises, you must change. You can try to delay it by clinging to old habits and attitudes, and you can always find reasons for putting it off until tomorrow. But be honest: Do you really want to stay the same when Jesus offers so much more?

Once I got past the initial resistance in my heart, I needed to overcome several other obstacles. The first is what I call tapping blue jays—the mental and emotional noise that pecks away at my resolve by distracting me. Just the other day, while I was working in my home office, there was a blue jay on my roof, banging away on an unshelled peanut he'd taken from the bird feeder on the back deck. It was the sort of tapping that can't be ignored, especially if you know the damage a jay's beak can do to a wood-shake roof. I had to get up from my desk and scare the bird away.

Tapping blue jays are any distractions that draw us away from what we should be doing. For me, it's the tendency to take the path of least resistance. Though some people regard me as highly motivated and disciplined, I realize such a perception is based on the part of me they see. I know there's another part they can't see—a part I don't want them to see. It's the part of me that puts off doing things I don't like to do until the last minute, even when there is a price to be paid for inaction.

Cindy observed this trait during the first few months of our marriage, while we were students at the University of Texas. After I had dropped a Greek class for the third time, she called me on it. I gave some lame excuse about getting behind because I was sick, but she saw through my cover-up and said, "The truth is, you're a lazy bum."

Looking back, I think she was partially right. I'm not a bum, but I can be lazy—especially when it comes to my spiritual life. Though I'm fairly consistent in the disciplines of prayer, Bible reading, and Scripture memorization, there's another side that resists any work involved in knowing Christ better. By that, I mean taking what I learn from the Bible and diligently applying it to my life. I'm painfully aware the religious leaders who opposed Jesus were well versed in the Old Testament. They took pride in their highly disciplined religious lives. But they didn't know God and hadn't integrated what they knew from the Scriptures into their lives. One of my fears as I approached the Jesus Experiment was that my laziness would prevail—that I would prove to be unwilling to cast aside the delays and distractions and do the daily work necessary to achieve the desired results.

Breaking Down Barriers

The point of this discussion isn't to identify all the potential barriers to the Jesus Experiment, whatever they may be for you. It's to discover how to break them down. For me, it took remembering how I had overcome laziness in the past.

For years, I avoided going to the gym and working out. By the time I reached my early thirties, I was in such bad shape that I could hardly bend over and touch my toes. Years of physical abuse from sports had taken a toll. Forced to choose between further deterioration and getting in shape, I decided to meet with my friend Lance Coffel, owner of River's Edge Athletic Club.

"I want to get in shape," I told him.

"How committed are you?"

"Totally," I said with the resolve of an army recruit.

"How much time will you give me?"

I stood tall, puffed out my chest, and said with confidence, "Fifteen minutes, two days a week."

Lance smiled and shook his head in disbelief. He then spent the next hour bringing every muscle in my body, including several I didn't know existed, to the point of total fatigue. When I finally shambled out to my car, my hands were shaking so badly I could hardly get the key into the slot to unlock the door.

For the next week, my entire body scolded me for abusing it. When the pain finally abated, I realized I faced two options: I could either stay in terrible shape or I could commit to working out for thirty minutes, three days a week. The first option didn't sound good, so I chose the better one. As I started regular workouts, something unexpected happened: I saw results, and that made me want to work out more. So I upped my workouts to forty-five minutes, and then an hour. Later I added another day per week to my workout routine. Decades have passed, and I've stuck with it.

The pain it took to overcome my laziness illustrates the psychological law of gravity: *A person will continue down a path of destructive behavior until the pain of continuing exceeds the pain of changing.* My suffering body convinced me I needed to get in shape. Knowing that not getting in shape was a worse option, I overcame the laziness that had anchored my will and kept me from moving forward.

A person will continue down a path of destructive behavior until the pain of continuing exceeds the pain of changing.

As I thought about the Jesus Experiment, the tapping blue jays reminded me it would require a level of spiritual effort I've often avoided. However, I was at a place in my spiritual journey similar to the day when Lance gave me that first workout. Not that I was out of shape, necessarily. But I didn't want to stay in the same place because it wasn't satisfying—it was more painful to remain stagnant than to move forward. I wanted to press on. I wanted to get closer to God and become more like Jesus. I wanted to know the joy of God's transforming work in my life. I would no longer be held back by tapping blue jays or my resistance to investing the effort needed to live the Jesus Experiment. I was all in.

Finding a Role Model

For some people, what it means to become more like Jesus is too abstract. After all, we're not walking with him in the flesh. Sometimes it's easier to see Jesus in other people—people who model Christian maturity. The apostle Paul offered himself as a role model to the Corinthians when he told them, "Follow my example, as I follow the example of Christ" (1 Corinthians 11:1). For me, that example was a man named Freeman Schmidt.

When I was in my early thirties, I moved from Texas to Oregon to become the lead pastor of a church in the Portland area. Freeman, who had previously pastored a thriving church in central Oregon for more than thirty years, was already on staff. He had a full head of white hair, a tender spirit, an ordered life, a loving wife, four children, and an ongoing joy. Most of all, he loved Jesus, and it showed.

As I got to know Freeman, I noticed how different he seemed from other older men. Curious about this, I brought it up one day. "Freeman, it seems that people get rigid and prickly as they get older. But you're gentler and"—I hesitated because I didn't want to seem flippant—"godlier. Why?"

Freeman smiled. "Bill, as people age, their true inner self pokes through to the outside. They don't have the strength to restrain themselves, so you see what they're really like."

His words fell into my mind like a seed, which quickly germinated and grew into an insight: I was in the presence of a true man of God. As Freeman continued to age over the next several years, I saw more of Jesus in him. He was the kind of man I wanted to become as I grew older.

One day, in late winter, Freeman told me he had a fast-growing brain tumor. He said it was terminal and inoperable. The doctors had told him that, as the tumor continued to grow, it would most likely be painless, he would sleep longer and longer each night, and one day he wouldn't wake up.

Sometimes it's easier to see Jesus in other people—people who model Christian maturity.

From Freeman's perspective, though this was bad news, it gave him time to get his affairs in order and express love to his family and friends. So Freeman spent the remaining months of his life straightening out his already immaculate garage, making sure his finances were settled, giving away his library, playing golf, and hanging out with people he loved. True to the doctor's prognosis, each night he slept a little longer.

I visited Freeman one day in his home, less than a week before he died. He was sleeping on his back, with a pillow under his head and a sheet and light blanket pulled up to his chest. His hands were folded over his stomach. I read to him from the Psalms, but I didn't know if he heard me. It didn't matter; I loved the man and cherished just being with him.

Before leaving, I stood at his bedside, placed my right hand on his hands, and prayed for him, my voice soft in the quiet room. When I finished, Freeman pulled my hand to his mouth. Thinking he was asleep and needed a tissue, I raised my hand and reached for a box of Kleenex. At that moment, Freeman gently, but with determination, pulled my hand to his mouth and kissed it.

I think of how Jesus honored his disciples on the night before his death by washing their feet.

He never opened his eyes or uttered a word. Yet with that silent gesture, he said all he could about his feelings for me. I leaned over, kissed his cheek, and told him I loved him.

Reflecting on that moment, I think of how Jesus honored his disciples on the night before his death by washing their feet. Too weak to wash my feet, Freeman kissed my hand. He did what I believe Jesus would have done if he had been lying on Freeman's bed, slowly slipping into death. And in doing that for me, Freeman nurtured my desire to become more like the Master we both served.

When I started the Jesus Experiment, I had Freeman in mind. I didn't know what the outcome of the twelve-week spiritual exercise would be, but I hoped it would move me along the road to being more like Freeman, and ultimately more like Jesus Christ.

As you begin the Jesus Experiment, I encourage you to look toward a role model for encouragement as you fix your eyes on the Master and seek to become more like him day by day.

Getting Started

When I decided to restart the Jesus Experiment, I wanted to devise a process that could be tried for a *limited* period of time—long enough to test the hypothesis and see if Jesus brings abundant life, but not so long it would be daunting and provide an excuse not to start.

I'm far more likely to continue doing something if I start light and slowly build to a rigorous effort—which is what I did with my workout routine. I also wanted something that would stretch my thinking and challenge me spiritually. So the Jesus Experiment became a twelve-week exercise, centered on one major truth about Jesus each week, based on the following four commitments:

1. *Ask* what Jesus felt, thought, said, and did in a variety of situations.
2. *Observe* your own responses in similar real-life situations by noting what you *feel, think, say,* and *do* when you are self-reliant.
3. *Evaluate* what you would *feel, think, say,* and *do* in the same circumstances if you were abiding in Jesus and following his example.
4. *Apply* a specific plan to *prepare* yourself to *actively* follow in Jesus' footsteps the next time you encounter similar circumstances. You might be tempted to skip this step, but it's the most important. Only through real, concrete steps of faith can we become more like Christ, experiencing the abundant life he offers.

Living the Jesus Experiment

Just as conducting an experiment in a lab is different from hearing a teacher lecture about scientific principles or studying them in a book, living the Jesus Experiment will take more than merely reading this book. In order to discover the validity of Jesus' promise of abundant life, you must diligently seek to discover how he felt, thought, spoke, and acted in specific situations, and then determine, by God's grace, to conform how you feel, think, speak, and act into his likeness. This will require effort on your part.

To start the experiment, take a moment to read John 10:1-10 below and answer the questions that follow.

"I tell you the truth, anyone who sneaks over the wall of a sheepfold, rather than going through the gate, must surely be a thief and a robber! But the one who enters through the gate is the shepherd of the sheep. The gatekeeper opens the gate for him, and the sheep recognize his voice and come to him. He calls his own sheep by name and leads them out. After he has gathered his own flock, he walks ahead of them, and they follow him because they know his voice. They won't follow a stranger; they will run from him because they don't know his voice."

Those who heard Jesus use this illustration didn't understand what he meant, so he explained it to them: "I tell you the truth, I am the gate for the sheep. All who came before me were thieves and robbers. But the true sheep did not listen to them. Yes, I am the gate. Those who come in through me will be saved. They will come and go freely and will find good pastures. The thief's purpose is to steal and kill and destroy. My purpose is to give them a rich and satisfying life." (NLT)

1. What do you hope to get from the Jesus Experiment? Take a moment and write your answer.

_____

_____

_____

_____

2. How did Jesus compare what he offers to what thieves and robbers do?

_____

_____

_____

_____

3. What do you think Jesus meant when he said he offers "a rich and satisfying life"?

_____

_____

_____

_____

4. What would such a life look like for you? How is your idea different or similar to what Jesus offers?

_____

_____

_____

_____

5. What fears could keep you from living the Jesus Experiment? How will you confront them?

_____

_____

_____

_____

6. What delays and distractions could keep you from living the Jesus Experiment? What will you do to break down those barriers?

_____

_____

_____

_____

7. What "tapping blue jays" will try to chip away at your resolve and urge you to take the path of least resistance? How will you overcome them?

_____

_____

_____

_____

8. If you're not studying this book in a small group, do you have a friend or two you could ask to live the Jesus Experiment with you? Make a plan to contact them.

_____

_____

_____

_____

9. How would living the Jesus Experiment with a friend help you?

_____

_____

_____

_____

To help you with the Jesus Experiment process, a chart will be provided at the end of each chapter to give you a place to record what you're learning.

What did Jesus . . .	What do I . . .	
Feel?	Feel when self-reliant?	Feel when abiding in Jesus?
Think?	Think when self-reliant?	Think when abiding in Jesus?
Say?	Say when self-reliant?	Say when abiding in Jesus?
Do?	Do when self-reliant?	Do when abiding in Jesus?

Abiding in Jesus

I GREW UP IN A CRAZY FAMILY.

Here's what I mean by crazy. My mother was fifteen when my father, who was twenty-four and married to her sister, got my mother pregnant. She gave birth to a girl. A little more than a year later, my mother had a second girl, again by my father. Two years after that, my dad divorced my aunt and married my mother. My parents then had another girl, followed by me. A year later, my little sister entered the world. My mother also had another daughter, with a different man, so I also have an older half-sister.

With such a horrid start, it's no surprise my parents hit some bumps over the course of their marriage. During my early childhood, they separated and placed my sisters and me in an orphanage. All I remember from those days is one of my sisters telling me I wouldn't have to brush my teeth as long as I wet the brush bristles.

That's one of my earliest memories, and I'm still trying to figure out its deeper meaning.

During her early twenties, my mother discovered vodka would ease her pain and replace it with a sense of well-being. Alcohol served as her drug of choice throughout much of her adult life. That changed when she was seriously injured in a car wreck and spent six months in the hospital. Vodka didn't make a dent in her new pain, but pain meds helped, so she exchanged one addiction for another.

My dad is a different story. I think he drank to muffle the sound of my mother's nagging. He made a lot of money selling life insurance to New Mexico and Texas oilmen and ranchers. But he always spent it faster than he made it. I recall him hosting barbecue and beer parties at our home for the high school football team. Wild nights.

Creating Drama

My parents fought nonstop. They divorced a couple of times but always got back together. I'm not sure why, except they must have liked the drama.

One night, my drunken mother slit her left wrist with a razor blade. I watched as one of my sisters struggled hysterically to take away the blade and apply a tourniquet to my mother's arm. Not an image I'll ever forget.

I recall my dad slapping my mother because she made a demeaning reference to his mother. Mom wore sunglasses the next day.

And then there was the night my mother brought home a guy she'd met at a bar. I was only nine, but I knew how to handle a gun. As she laughed in the kitchen with her "date," I marched into my parent's bedroom and grabbed my dad's shotgun out of the closet, walked back to the kitchen, and told the guy to get out or I'd shoot him. The gun wasn't loaded, but he didn't ask. He left.

We occasionally went to church, but I felt as out of place as a beggar at a formal dinner. At the time, I thought all church people lived good, moral lives, free of profanity, dishonesty, lust, anger, and the other misdeeds that defined my life. I also thought they were born that way and that's why they went to church. They were good people telling other good people how to be better people.

I thought all church people lived good, moral lives, free of profanity, dishonesty, lust, anger, and the other misdeeds that defined my life.

The church gave me a Bible, and I spent enough time reading it to know I had to change or suffer the wrath of God. That realization prompted me to try to clean up my act. With my best friend, Ben Smith, I decided to stop cussing. I lived a profanity-free life that night and part of the following morning. I would have made it longer if not for Virgil Lewis. During PE he slammed my shin with a field hockey stick. I not only broke my no-swearing vow many times over, I also hit Virgil in the mouth and landed in the principal's office.

By the ninth grade, I knew I couldn't reform myself into a better person. So I pretended to be better. But no matter how hard I tried to be nice, I kept hurting the people I loved the most. Finally, when I was eighteen, my insensitivity triggered a crisis that drove me to my knees. I cried out to God, pleading with him to save me from myself. Seeking guidance, I got involved in a campus ministry at the University of Texas. Six months later, I understood that Christ had died to pay for my sins and had been raised from the dead. I'd heard that before but never realized he was punished in my place and that I only needed to accept his payment by faith (Ephesians 2:8-9).

This truth made sense. I knew I could never live a good enough life to earn God's favor. So I decided to trust Jesus. Immediate and noticeable changes took place. I quit stealing and swearing, and I believed I was on the path to lasting reformation. Yet deep-rooted character flaws don't just disappear, even when someone decides to follow Christ. I grew for a year and then got mad at God for not rewarding my spiritual devotion. Not knowing how to process the disappointment, I did what I had learned from my parents: I medicated my pain with drugs.

A year later, stoned on psilocybin, I had a psychotic break. Fortunately, that terrifying experience convinced me Satan is real and I needed to take God seriously or my life would self-destruct. Holding on to my sanity by a thread, I accepted Jesus' invitation to those who are weary and burdened to come to him for rest (Matthew 11:28-29).

Deep-rooted character flaws don't just disappear, even when someone decides to follow Christ.

Decades have passed, and I'm amazed by the changes Christ has made in my life. Nothing astonishes me more than the fact that, in almost forty years of marriage, I've never said something that deeply hurt my wife. Don't misunderstand me—we've had our share of arguments. But before I knew Christ, I used my tongue to inflict deep wounds on those I loved.

I've still got a long way to go, as my family and friends will no doubt affirm. Some of my old habits, like swearing, occasionally return. I also realize I'm only one step away from the first in a series of steps that could lead to my downfall.

Two Questions

My experience proves that Jesus can change a person, regardless of childhood traumas or destructive psychological and behavioral issues. It also raises two important questions. First, how is it possible for a believer to fall morally so far and so fast? Second, what does Jesus teach us that will prevent such a fall or that will pick us up when we stumble? To put it differently, what does Jesus teach us that will enable us to live an abundant life in his power?

As we'll see in the next chapter, Jesus set aside the exercise of his divine powers during his earthly life. He modeled for us not only what God would look like if he came to earth, but also what we would look like if we walked in total dependence on God. The power he displayed flowed from God the Father through him to accomplish the Father's purpose. That same power is available to us as God's children.

It's crucial for us to remember that when we come to faith in Jesus Christ, God fundamentally changes our nature. He turns sinners, who live apart from him, into saints, who live *in* him. He transforms creeping caterpillars into flying butterflies. All who believe in Jesus become identified with him in his death, burial, and resurrection. This spiritual reality forms the basis of our new and true identity. Everything that's true of Jesus (apart from his nontransferable divine attributes, such as omniscience, omnipotence, and omnipresence, which he reassumed upon his ascension into heaven) is true of us. We're in Christ, like pages in a book. What's true of the book is true of the pages.

> *Jesus modeled for us not only what God would look like if he came to earth, but also what we would look like if we walked in total dependence on God.*

That's why Paul said, "I have been crucified with Christ and I no longer live, but Christ lives in me. The life I live in the body, I live by faith in the Son of God, who loved me and gave himself for me" (Galatians 2:20).

We possess the same resources that Jesus did to help us live godly lives (as Jesus did).

Of course, we still have to deal with sinful appetites. But those appetites don't define our true identity. Christ does. Consider these truths:

- We are new creatures in Christ (2 Corinthians 5:17).
- We possess the mind of Christ (1 Corinthians 2:16).
- We are partakers of the divine nature without being divine ourselves (2 Peter 1:4).
- We possess the Spirit of God and Christ lives in us through the Holy Spirit (1 John 3:24).
- Because we are in Christ, we should live as he lived (1 John 2:6).

How does someone who possesses new life in Christ fall back into a destructive and sinful lifestyle like I did? If we're "new creatures" and set free, why does any believer ever sin?

The answer has to do with the fact that when we come to faith in Christ, we receive the Holy Spirit (Ephesians 4:30) but still possess what the Bible calls the "flesh" (Romans 8:3, ESV). The flesh is the part of us that craves gratification and pleasure apart from God. As long as we live in our bodies, we'll battle our fleshly tendencies. The point of the Jesus Experiment is to learn how to "become partakers of the divine nature" (2 Peter 1:4, ESV) and become more like Jesus.

You, too, have learned sinful and ineffective coping and communication techniques. Every person and every family is broken in some way.

For much of my life, I lived according to the flesh—that is, the part of me that lives independent of God. During those years, I used coping mechanisms, such as alcohol, sex, and drugs, to medicate my pain. I also related to other people according to destructive techniques learned from my family.

Though you may not come from a family as messed up as mine, you, too, have learned sinful and ineffective coping and communication techniques. Every person and every family is broken in some way. Because we've practiced these techniques for so many years, they've become our fallback thinking and acting mechanisms.

As a new believer and an immature nineteen-year-old, when faced with a crisis, I reacted from my flesh and reverted to the destructive patterns of my past. It surprised me the first time it happened because, for the most part, I had walked in the power of Christ for a year. I had no idea evil was so alive within me. Regrettably, that experience reinforced the view I had of myself prior to believing in Christ. I thought my evil thoughts, desires, and destructive behavior defined me.

At the time, I didn't know about my new identity in Christ or how to live in his power. And yet, this truth is so central to life in Christ that Jesus explained it to his disciples the night before his death. Carrying out his mission would require understanding their future relationship with him and how to tap into his strength. Such insight enables us to live the abundant life Jesus promised.

The Jesus Experiment

What did Jesus feel and think?

As I wrote this chapter, it occurred to me it's unlike any that follow. In each of the remaining chapters, we'll see how Jesus responded in a variety of settings. For instance, we'll note how he faced fear and temptation and how he interacted with vulnerable and difficult people. We'll examine what he felt and thought in the face of those challenges, and we'll compare ourselves to him.

Here, however, the focus is on what he taught his disciples the night before his crucifixion, when he explained to them the central principle of abundant living—namely, abiding in him. Jesus certainly felt the entire range of human emotions as he encountered temptation, opposition, fear, suffering, and every other human experience—just as we do. But through it all, one truth remained constant: Despite how he felt, Jesus always chose to abide in and rely on his Father.

Time and again, Jesus declared that his power came from God. He wanted his disciples to understand this so that one day they would draw strength from him, just as he drew strength from his Father.

During Jesus' final meal with his disciples, Philip asked him to show them the Father. Jesus answered, "Don't you believe that I am in the Father, and that the Father is in me? The words I say to you are not just my own. Rather, it is the Father, living in me, who is doing his work. Believe me when I say that I am in the Father and the Father is in me" (John 14:10-11). No matter what Jesus felt or thought, it's clear he always depended on his Father for wisdom and strength.

Once we acknowledge this, we can use what Jesus felt and thought on that final night as an example of the kind of feelings he dealt with as he depended on God. With that in mind, before the disciples ate the Passover meal, we're told Jesus was "troubled in spirit" (John 13:21). The word for "troubled" speaks of someone whose emotions are stirred up. It was the word used to describe how Jesus felt at the grave of Lazarus when he saw Mary weeping—just before he cried.

Jesus felt the entire range of human emotions as he encountered temptation, opposition, fear, suffering, and every other human experience.

In the upper room, as Jesus talked with the men he loved, he knew that, in a short time, Judas would betray him, the disciples would abandon him, Peter would deny him, and the Romans and Jews would arrest, try, and crucify him. Not only would Jesus suffer, but so would his disciples as they grieved his death and their own cowardice. In the face of emotions stirred up by such thoughts, Jesus emphasized that his leaving would be to their advantage.

They must have wondered how the absence of the man who spoke words of wisdom, healed the sick, raised the dead, and claimed to be the promised Messiah could possibly be to their advantage. The Lord's answer shows he had been thinking about this evening for some time. He told them that if he didn't leave, he couldn't send the Counselor—the Holy Spirit (John 16:7), who would always be with them (whereas, Jesus implies, in his earthly body, he could only be in one place at a time).

This change would usher in a new age. In the Old Testament era, believers weren't permanently indwelt by the Holy Spirit. He provided some of them with temporary abilities to carry out God's work. He gave physical power to Samson, divine revelation to the prophets, wisdom to Solomon, and enablement to perform miracles to Moses, Elijah, and Elisha—to name some notable instances.

After Jesus ascended to the right hand of the Father in heaven and the Holy Spirit came on the day of Pentecost, every Christian would possess God's Spirit. This indwelling occurs at the moment of spiritual rebirth. That's why Paul said, "You did not receive a spirit that makes you a slave again to fear, but you received the Spirit of sonship. And by him we cry, 'Abba, Father'" (Romans 8:15).

The moment we trust in Jesus, God's Spirit acts like an electric current touching the filament of our spirit, and we're able to fulfill our God-given purpose.

Just as we possess the physical DNA of our human father, we possess the spiritual DNA of our heavenly Father. The moment we accepted Jesus, the Spirit of God placed the life of Christ within us. We now possess a new kind of life, which expresses itself through godly thoughts and actions. That's our true self.

What did Jesus say and do?

Jesus' words and deeds on the night of the Last Supper were focused on helping the disciples grasp a truth as revolutionary as the first use of incandescent light. "On that day you will realize that I am in my Father, and you are in me, and I am in you" (John 14:20).

In a sense, each one of us is like a lightbulb—an airtight glass bulb housing a tungsten filament. When the bulb is connected to a power supply, the electric current zips through the tungsten, releasing the light photons. A lightbulb cannot fulfill its intended purpose without electricity. When the power goes out, a lightbulb generates no more light than an empty glass jar. But the moment the power returns, the bulb glows again. Similarly, our body is the glass bulb and our spirit is the filament. The moment we trust in Jesus, God's Spirit acts like an electric current touching the filament of our spirit, and we're able to fulfill our God-given purpose.[1]

Unlike the unreliable power source on which a lightbulb depends, the Holy Spirit indwells us with an inexhaustible and unbreakable supply of energy—the same resource that Jesus drew upon during his life on earth. The question is, how do we follow his example and draw on such wisdom and strength? Jesus answered that question with one word: *abide*.

After leaving the upper room and leading his disciples out of Jerusalem, Jesus paused at a vineyard, took a grapevine in his hand, and said,

> *I am the true vine, and my Father is the vinedresser. Every branch in me that does not bear fruit he takes away, and every branch that does bear fruit he prunes, that it may bear more fruit. Already you are clean because of the word that I have spoken to you.* Abide *in me, and I in you. As the branch cannot bear fruit by itself, unless it* abides *in the vine, neither can you, unless you* abide *in me. I am the vine; you are the branches. Whoever* abides *in me and I in him, he it is that bears much fruit, for apart from me you can do nothing. If anyone does not* abide *in me he is thrown away like a branch*

and withers; and the branches are gathered, thrown into the fire, and burned. If you abide *in me, and my words* abide *in you, ask whatever you wish, and it will be done for you. By this my Father is glorified, that you bear much fruit and so prove to be my disciples. As the Father has loved me, so have I loved you.* Abide *in my love. If you keep my commandments, you will* abide *in my love, just as I have kept my Father's commandments and* abide *in his love. These things I have spoken to you, that my joy may be in you, and that your joy may be full. (John 15:1-11,* ESV, *emphasis added)*

Jesus could have told his followers that the key to victorious and joyful living involves performing a religious ritual, abstaining from certain foods or drinks, giving money to help the poor, or attending church. Instead he repeated that single word—*abide*—ten times, so the disciples, and we, wouldn't miss the point.

The essence of abiding is staying connected and allowing the life of the vine to produce its natural fruit through us. All our striving and struggling and seeking dissolve in that one quiet verb: *abide.* That's how we prove to be his disciples. That's how we become more like him. And that's the essence of the Jesus Experiment.

When Jesus spoke of bearing much fruit, I believe he was talking about the fruit of the Spirit—namely love, joy, peace, patience, kindness, goodness, faithfulness, gentleness, and self-control (Galatians 5:22-23). When those nine qualities become evident in our lives, we know we're becoming more like Jesus.

What I feel and think

The imagery of the vine is profound in its simplicity. Just as a branch draws nourishment from the vine to bear edible fruit, so we draw from Jesus all we need to bear spiritual fruit. It's as if, when we become Christians, God attaches a spiritual umbilical cord to our spirits so he can impart to us his life and strength. Unlike a physical birth, when the doctor cuts the cord, in our spiritual rebirth, God remains attached to us.[2]

Of course, we can twist or pinch the cord so God's nourishment and strength don't reach us. But all his resources are still available. When they flow from his Spirit through us, they produce the fruit of the Spirit in our feelings, thoughts, words, and deeds.

Just as a branch draws nourishment from the vine to bear edible fruit, so we draw from Jesus all we need to bear spiritual fruit.

Our job is simply to abide in Christ—to live in a state of relaxed reliance upon him. His job is to transform us into his image. Initially, such faith is a conscious act. When you catch yourself feeling irritable, lustful, ungrateful, or impatient, you must pause and recognize such feelings can lead to attitudes and actions that don't flow from Christ. When you feel that way, you need to let your emotions serve as a reminder you're not abiding in the Vine. Then you must engage your mind and confess to God that you're not abiding in Jesus, and by faith thank him that Jesus still lives in you.

There will be times when you won't feel like taking such a step. That's when you need to act in faith, regardless of what your emotions are telling you. Over time, reading your emotions and shifting your thinking back to a focus on Jesus will become more spontaneous, much like the practiced movements of a concert pianist or an Olympic gymnast.

What I say and do

Fortunately for us, Jesus told his disciples something they could do to facilitate their abiding in him: *internalize his words.* He said, "If you abide in me, *and my words abide in you*, ask whatever you wish, and it will be done for you" (John 15:7, ESV, emphasis added).

As we'll see in chapter 5, when we look at the temptation of Jesus, Jesus had so internalized the Word of God that he could draw on it to expose Satan's lies and resist his enticements. Time and again, Jesus referred from memory to the teachings of the Old Testament.

Over the years, I've made Bible meditation and memorization a part of my daily routine. I've found this practice has enabled me to speak the truth of God's Word into situations where it was needed.

Because the words of the Bible express the mind of God, when we read it, meditate on it, and memorize it, we infuse our mind, soul, and spirit with the thoughts of God. It recently occurred to me that the Scriptures are a visible expression of the invisible God. When we hide it in our hearts, it becomes invisible again. Once within us, the invisible words of God are energized by the Holy Spirit to produce obedience.

Because the words of the Bible express the mind of God, when we read it, meditate on it, and memorize it, we infuse our mind, soul, and spirit with the thoughts of God.

Jesus addressed another important topic while talking about abiding. He said, "If you keep my commandments, you will abide in my love, just as I have kept my Father's commandments and abide in his love" (John 15:10, ESV).

Just as children live within the protective love of their parents by obeying them, so we live in God's protective love when we obey him.

Abiding in Jesus consists of three elements:

- Living in a state of relaxed reliance on him
- Meditating on God's Word so it abides in us and through it we abide in him
- Obeying the commands of God so we abide in his love

As we'll see in the following chapters, Jesus' private life prepared him to live in a way that honored his Father. That same life is available to us as we learn to abide in Christ.

The Power to Change

I began this chapter by telling you I grew up in an unhealthy family. I did that so you would know the power of Christ is available to everyone, regardless of family history. But I had another reason for telling the story. I wanted to give you hope that, as Christ works in and through you, he will also affect those close to you.

After I became a Christ follower, so did the rest of my family. And though God didn't wave a wand and heal every wound, he did begin changing us. My sisters' lives of faith astound me. I cherish them, as well as the memory of my parents.

A few weeks ago, I was reminded of how profoundly the Lord worked in my mother's life. While looking for a book in my library, I found the first Bible I ever owned. Published in 1967, *Good News for Modern Man* was a paraphrased edition of the New Testament. As I flipped through the underlined and highlighted pages, I found something I had forgotten. On a blank page in the front of the Bible, I had written:

Happy birthday, Mom,

You can have my Bible. May the Lord show you as much in this Bible as he did me.

Love in Christ,
Bill

Reading those words, I felt I had discovered a hidden treasure. And then I came across these words, written in my mother's handwriting:

Ryan Perkins,

This little book belonged to your father when he was about your age. He gave it to me to keep—now I wish to pass it on to you with the prayers that you will also learn God's ways (heart). Many people know God's works (acts), but not his ways.

Love in Christ,
Grandma 11/5/92

Remembering how broken my mother had been, I marveled at this visible reminder of the powerful work of Christ in her life. As we live the Jesus Experiment, I'm convinced that not only will *we* be changed by God's power, so will the people we love.

Living the Jesus Experiment

This Week

Every time you're tempted to rely on your own strength, wisdom, or initiative, ask God what Jesus would feel, think, say, and do in the same situation. Now take note of your own responses. What are you feeling, thinking, saying, and doing? Pray God will enable you to follow in the steps of Jesus by abiding in him.

Ask

Read John 14:25-26; 15:1-10. On the chart on page 35, examine the left-hand column, noting what Jesus felt, thought, said, and did. Put a check by the statements that are true.

    ____ If you try hard enough, you can please God.

    ____ The same resources that were available to Christ are there for you.

____ Living an abundant life results from relying on Christ to live through you.

____ It's impossible for Christians to stumble morally.

According to John 15:4-9, what three elements are involved in abiding in Christ?

_____

_____

_____

_____

_____

In John 15:4-10, why does Jesus repeat the word *abide* ten times? Why is abiding so important?

_____

_____

_____

_____

Observe

Briefly describe a specific, recent situation in your life where you tended to be self-reliant rather than abiding in Christ. Fill in the center column of the chart (p. 35), recording how you felt, thought, spoke, and acted in that situation.

_____

_____

_____

_____

_____

_____

Evaluate

Fill in the right-hand column of the chart, recording how you believe you would feel, think, speak, and act in that same situation if you were abiding in Jesus.

Apply

On the lines below, write specific steps you'll take to prepare yourself for the next time you have to choose between self-reliance and Christ-dependence. Spend a few minutes in prayer, asking God to guide you.

_____

_____

_____

_____

_____

_____

Here are a few ideas to get you started:

- Meditate on a verse that helps you remember the importance of abiding in Christ. Here are two good ones: "I am the vine, you are the branches; he who abides in Me and I in him, he bears much fruit, for apart from Me you can do nothing" (John 15:5, NASB); "I have been crucified with Christ and I no longer live, but Christ lives in me. The life I now live in the body, I live by faith in the Son of God, who loved me and gave himself for me" (Galatians 2:20).
- Write what you'll think and say to express an abiding faith in Christ. You might say something like this: "Father, I admit my words and behavior show I'm living in my own power,

not Christ's. Right now, I choose to depend on Jesus to produce the fruit of the Spirit through me. Thank you that, according to his promise, I will bear much fruit as I abide in him by faith."

- Practice how you'll change your thoughts to express an abiding faith.
- Place a reminder on a frequently viewed surface, such as a counter top, mirror, or computer screen.
- Discuss abiding in Christ with a friend or your small group.

One Week Later

Record your thoughts about how living the Jesus Experiment helped you abide in Jesus during the past seven days. How has abiding in Christ made your life more fulfilling and joyful?

_____

_____

_____

_____

_____

_____

_____

_____

_____

_____

_____

_____

_____

_____

_____

_____

_____

REGARDING EMPOWERMENT		
What did Jesus . . .	**What do I . . .**	
Feel? Though the Bible doesn't state what Jesus felt, it seems he would have felt concern for his disciples with confidence in his Father to provide all they needed to live a victorious life. (John 14:20-21, 24-26, 15:1-10)	*Feel when self-reliant?*	*Feel when abiding in Jesus?*
Think? Jesus was thinking about how he could communicate to his disciples the nature of their relationship once he was absent. (John 17:18-23)	*Think when self-reliant?*	*Think when abiding in Jesus?*
Say? Jesus told the disciples to abide in him as a branch abides in a vine, in order to bear much fruit. Abiding involved meditating on his words and obeying his commands. (John 15:7-10)	*Say when self-reliant?*	*Say when abiding in Jesus?*
Do? He took them to a vineyard and talked about how, as a branch abides in a vine, they should abide in him. (John 15:1-11)	*Do when self-reliant?*	*Do when abiding in Jesus?*

Download full-size charts and study questions at www.jesusexperiment.com.

What Jesus Did in Private

He Talked with His Father

WHAT HAPPENS BEHIND the scenes makes all the difference for a concert pianist, an Olympic gymnast, an artist, an author, or anyone else exceptionally skilled at something. According to Malcolm Gladwell in his book *Outliers,* it takes ten thousand hours of practice for someone to reach the level of a world-class expert.

Even Mozart had to practice to achieve greatness. Though he composed his first concertos for piano and orchestra when he was seven, they aren't considered very good and most were arrangements of other composers' work. Indeed, his father may have done most of the composing for him.

Music critic Harold Schonberg claims that Mozart developed late and didn't produce his greatest work until he had been composing for twenty years.[3]

Gladwell illustrates the ten-thousand-hour rule by referring to bands, businessmen, computer programmers, chess masters, musicians, and hockey players. Yes, the Beatles practiced or played for ten thousand hours before they ever hit the big time. Bill Gates commented about the time he spent sharpening his computer programming skills while in high school. He said, "It would be a rare week that we wouldn't get twenty or thirty hours in."[4] Apparently, it takes that many hours for the brain to learn all it needs to know for world-class expertise.

The Power of Private Practice

I mention the ten-thousand-hour rule because it illustrates the fact that what someone does well in public is the result of private practice. Research indicates that even someone less innately talented can become a world-class expert if he or she works harder, much harder, than everyone else. With enough practice, a difficult task can be made to look simple—like a gold medal performance in Olympic figure skating.

All of this makes me wonder how much time Jesus must have spent in private prayer by the time he launched his public ministry at age thirty. We don't know much about his childhood and young adulthood, but when he finally stepped into the public eye, he lived with such godly wisdom, power, and grace that it's safe to assume he spent countless hours with his Father, learning what God wanted him to say and do. Every word he spoke, every miracle he performed, flowed from what he did in private. Jesus had mastered the heart of his Father.

Nothing Jesus did was more important than the conversations he had in private with his Father.

Nothing Jesus did was more important than the conversations he had in private with his Father. Prayer was the conduit through which the Father's power and wisdom flowed into and through the

Son. If the purpose of the Jesus Experiment is for us to become more like Christ by abiding in him, we must start by imitating his prayer life.

Follow Jesus in Prayer

Imitating Jesus in prayer might sound as improbable as emulating Superman's flying capabilities. We might shadow Clark Kent up a flight of stairs, but we're not going to follow the Man of Steel off a tall building. Likewise, I suspect most people figure they could at least try to imitate Jesus when he operated from his human nature, but no way could they follow his lead when he relied on his divine nature.

Such thinking is based on the belief that Jesus flipped from one nature to the other, like a divine Transformer. While weeping at the grave of Lazarus, he utilized his human nature. When raising Lazarus from the dead, he acted from his divine nature. He taught from his human side, walked on water from his divine side.

I think such a view is inaccurate. At no time during his earthly ministry did Jesus tap into his divine power to know or do anything.[5] Instead, he always operated out of his humanity.

I've heard Bible scholars say Jesus performed miracles to prove he was God. The Bible doesn't tell us that, though. In fact, the Old Testament records that Moses, Elijah, and

Although Jesus was fully God, he laid aside all use of his divine attributes when he became a man.

Elisha performed miracles; and in New Testament times, Paul and Peter also performed miracles. None of these men claimed to be God, nor did they claim to be the source of their miraculous power. Instead, their miracles validated their claims that they spoke for God. And though Jesus did claim to be God (John 10:30-33), he never claimed the power he used to perform miracles came from himself.

Paul makes it clear that, although Jesus was fully God, he laid aside all use of his divine attributes when he became a man (see Philippians 2:5-8). Paul doesn't say Jesus laid aside his divinity, only that he laid aside the use of his divine attributes. God cannot cease being God, but he can waive the use of his divine powers.

For example, we could choose to lay aside our ability to see by keeping our eyes closed. We'd still possess good eyesight, but we wouldn't be using it. That's what Jesus did with his divine attributes: He chose not to use them while on earth.

Throughout his ministry, Jesus affirmed the source of his strength. In John 5:19-20, he declares his reliance on God the Father: "I tell you the truth, the Son can do nothing by himself; he can do only what he sees his Father doing, because whatever the Father does the Son also does. For the Father loves the Son and shows him all he does. Yes, to your amazement he will show him even greater things."

In John 5:30, Jesus says, "By myself I can do nothing." In John 14:9, he tells Philip, "Anyone who has seen me has seen the Father."

The same resources that enabled Jesus to live a life devoted to God are available to you and me.

In Matthew 24:36, he shows a human limitation of knowledge when he says he doesn't know the time of his return. Later, he notes that he could ask his Father to send twelve legions of angels to his aid, rather than commanding them himself (Matthew 26:53).

On the Day of Pentecost, after Jesus' death and resurrection, Peter spoke of the source of Jesus' power when he said, "Listen to this: Jesus of Nazareth was a man accredited by God to you by miracles, wonders and signs, *which God did among you through him*, as you yourselves know" (Acts 2:22, emphasis added).

This is a poignant truth. Why? Because the same resources that enabled Jesus to live a life devoted to God are available to you and me. As Jesus abided in the Father, so can we abide in Jesus. The Lord promised this when he said, "Anyone who has faith in me will do what I have been doing. He will do even greater things than these, because I am going to the Father" (John 14:12).

We could be men and women who show God to the world in the same way as Jesus. Yes, Jesus was fully God *and* fully man, but his words and actions flowed from his Father—and so can ours.

Of course, Jesus never struggled with internal sin and the destructive feelings, thoughts, words, and actions that sin produces. But he dealt with human emotions, physical needs, and difficult people, just as we do today. He relied on his Father and the power of the Holy Spirit—and so can we. Jesus spoke of our union with him and the Father when he said, "I pray that they will all be one, just as you and I are one—as you are in me, Father, and I am in you. And may they be in us so that the world will believe you sent me" (John 17:21, NLT).

As we live the Jesus Experiment, it's important to realize that we are able, in the power of the Holy Spirit, to feel,

We are able, in the power of the Holy Spirit, to feel, think, speak, and act like Jesus.

think, speak, and act like Jesus. The key is discovering why Jesus talked with his Father in private and then learning how he prayed.

Struggling to Pray

I have a recurring dream in which I'm running as hard as I can. Sometimes, I'm running barefoot across an open field of green grass in the country. Other times, I'm on an asphalt street in a crowded neighborhood. Often, I'm playing football and trying to outrun defenders.

What makes this dream troubling isn't *where* I'm running but *how*. The common denominator of all these dreams is that, although I'm running hard, I'm running slowly—as if the ground were covered with glue and I have to struggle just to lift my feet.

When I wake from these dreams, I feel weak—not with physical weakness, but with the weakness of my humanity. That's often how I feel when I think about prayer. I want to enjoy prayer like a fleet-footed runner enjoys a race. But when I pray, I'm slowed by the weight of my laziness and the tapping of distractions. And then I feel guilty because I haven't prayed long enough, or often enough, or with enough fervency.

I think most people share my feelings about prayer, including the disciples. In Gethsemane, Peter, James, and John repeatedly fell asleep while Jesus prayed. This was right after Jesus had confided in them, "My soul is crushed with grief to the point of death. Stay here and keep watch with me" (Mark 14:34, NLT).

Both the way Jesus prayed and the effects of his prayers stood in contrast with what the disciples had seen from other religious leaders.

If I feel guilty for not praying on a normal day, how must the disciples have felt after falling asleep in Gethsemane?

Throughout their time with Jesus, the disciples had not only seen him slip away to pray, but they had also heard him pray throughout the day. Both the way Jesus prayed and the effects of his prayers stood in contrast with what the disciples had seen from other religious leaders. By comparison, watching the Pharisees make a show of their prayers would have been like watching a troupe of actors performing for each other in front of mirrors.

The Private Prayers of Jesus

The prayers Jesus prayed were authentic and personal. Even when he prayed publicly, his words expressed an intimate familiarity with God. And he often prayed when alone. He did this to receive comfort, insight, guidance, and strength from his Father.

The four Gospels include a number of references to Jesus' private prayer life.

- He often slipped away to the wilderness to pray (Luke 5:16).
- He prayed in the morning before a busy day of ministry (Mark 1:35).
- After feeding the five thousand, and before he walked on water, he went up on a mountainside to pray (Mark 6:46).
- He prayed all night before calling his disciples (Luke 6:12-16).
- He prayed alone before asking his disciples, "Who do people say I am?" (Luke 9:18, NLT).
- He prayed alone before the disciples asked him to teach them to pray (Luke 11:1).
- In Gethsemane, before his arrest, Jesus prayed alone with Peter, James, and John nearby (Mark 14:32-42).

Solitude Erases Distractions

In our busy modern Western culture, solitude isn't a companion we seek. Though we may occasionally get away from other people, we're seldom free of distracting sounds and images. We've become addicted to the constant stimulation of texting, surfing, tweeting, and talking on cell phones, not to mention the Internet, television, radio, and iPods, iPads, and iPhones.

I recently visited a friend in his home for the first time. He greeted me warmly, and we walked into his den. The first thing I noticed was the forty-two-inch HDTV on the wall. Its screen flashed a colorful and precise image while the surround-sound speaker system delivered crisp highs and a chest-thumping bass line.

Because I hadn't come over to watch a sporting event or movie, I assumed he would turn off the TV, or at least mute the sound while we talked. He didn't. Instead, his head swiveled back and forth as he gazed at the TV and glanced at me. After a few minutes, I concluded he didn't want to talk, and so I gave up trying and waited until the next commercial to slip away.

Reflecting on that experience, I realize I often pray the same way. I carry on an unfocused conversation with God, in which I'm distracted by my vibrating cell phone, the conversation my wife is having in the other room, or the e-mail that just appeared on my computer screen.

The purpose of solitude is to erase distractions, so we can focus on talking to God and listening for his guidance, comfort, and wisdom.

The purpose of solitude is to *erase* distractions, like doodles from a page, so we can focus on what's really important—talking to God and listening for his guidance, comfort, and wisdom. I've learned that the simple act of kneeling on the floor and closing my eyes forces me to abandon distractions. Or I may listen to worship music or walk to a secluded spot.

Though Jesus didn't have to contend with the profusion of electronic distractions we experience in our culture, it's not as if his life was without distractions. He lived in a highly relational culture, and people swarmed him, soaking in his wisdom and seeking his touch. As his fame spread, he became like a modern-day celebrity followed by adoring crowds. At one point, his disciples sought him out and said, "Everyone is looking for you!" (Mark 1:37). Yet somehow Jesus managed to slip away to quiet places to pray. Whether it was early in the morning or late at night, he sought and found solitude.

Jesus lived with an ongoing awareness of his need for the Father's wisdom and strength.

In each instance when Jesus prayed alone, he faced a different kind of need that would require the wisdom and strength of his Father. It explains why Jesus not only prayed alone, but also uttered short prayers throughout the day. He lived with an ongoing awareness of his need for the Father's wisdom and strength.

I have to confess that I seldom feel such a need unless I'm faced with a serious problem. In times of crisis, I pray more because I know the challenge towers over me like a fire-breathing dragon. Because I know I need God's help, I cry out to him. Just let me, or a family member or friend, encounter a financial setback, a relational breakdown, physical pain, or a life-threatening diagnosis, and I'm compelled to pray.

When my oldest son, Ryan, called and said, "Dad, I've got bad news," I inhaled deeply.

"What's wrong?"

"I've got testicular cancer."

"You're sure?"

"I'm sure," he said.

When I got off the phone, I felt a deep need to talk with God. Too often, it takes a crisis to make us realize life is as fragile as a spider's web.[†] Such a realization drives us to our knees because we know we desperately need God. The truth is, we need his help all the time, just as we need air and water. But somehow we live most days as if we don't, carrying on in a state of practical atheism.

> *The more we embrace the reality that without God we are spiritually empty, the more we'll seek to talk to him in solitude and silence so he can fill us with his wisdom and strength.*

Amazingly, Jesus lived every moment in complete dependence on the Father. He always felt a need for his Father's wisdom. Those feelings were shaped by his awareness of his human need for divine guidance and strength.

That's why Jesus said, "By myself I can do nothing" (John 5:29).

[†] Fortunately, testicular cancer is one of the more treatable forms of cancer, if caught early. Ryan underwent surgery and radiation treatment and is now cancer-free and the father of two children.

The more we embrace the reality that without God we are spiritually empty, the more we'll seek to talk to him in solitude and silence so he can fill us with his wisdom and strength.

The Jesus Experiment

Knowing that Jesus never tapped into his divine nature but relied on the Father to work through his humanity makes me hungry for that kind of relationship with God. To even begin to approach that level of intimate dependence on God, we must learn to pray in private as Jesus did.

What did Jesus feel and think?

What compelled Jesus to seek such an intimate life of prayer with the Father? What was he thinking and feeling? I suppose someone could say that the emotion of the moment prompted him to pray—his concern, anger, fear, disappointment, joy, grief, or love.

The feeling that drove Jesus to seek private times of prayer was a sense of his human inadequacy.

In a sense that's true. But I believe there was a deeper feeling behind those emotions. At the core of his being, Jesus knew his human limitations. He recognized that he possessed too little knowledge to know what to do in every situation. He knew he lacked the strength needed to shepherd the people and fulfill his purpose.

The feeling that drove Jesus to seek private times of prayer was a deep sense of his human inadequacy. Not the inadequacy of a drug addict too weak to fight for his freedom or an abused woman afraid to stand up to her husband. He simply knew, with absolute certainty, that without the Father he was as incomplete as a bird without wings.

What I feel and think

One day, when I was in high school, I was sitting behind the wheel of my tank-like black-and-white Pontiac with my girlfriend at my side. We were enjoying a burger at a local hangout on Barton Springs Road when four guys in a turquoise-and-white classic '57 Chevy pulled in next to us. I felt a rush of anger as I noticed them checking out my girlfriend. When two of them climbed out of their car and approached us, I started my engine and slinked away.

In that moment, I felt as inadequate as a Chihuahua attacked by a pack of wolves. But though I lacked the strength to stand up to four guys on my own, I had friends who would back me up. Five minutes later, I returned, followed by a car filled with six bodyguards. I pulled my Pontiac beside the Chevy, and my buddies parked behind it—boxing them in. My friends got out of their car and asked the suddenly silent guys in the Chevy to find another place to hassle people.

I look back on that experience as an example of how I *should* feel about my need for God and the power available to me. If I truly understood my desperate need for his wisdom, strength, and grace, I would run to him like I ran to my friends. And if I really believed in the surpassing power of prayer, I'd ask for his help as quickly as I asked my friends.

It's not as if I don't pray. In fact, several years ago I prayed for an hour every day of the year. I walked to Cooks Butte Park, a wilderness park on the summit of the hill where we lived. Though the hill was covered with towering fir trees, the western slope had a lookout point with an unobstructed view of the Willamette Valley and the Oregon Coast Range in the distance.

I recall watching as the setting sun, a huge, glowing, unpeeled orange, slowly rested on the shoulders of a distant mountain. As it rolled over the horizon, it kissed the sky with a flush of reds, pinks, purples, and blues. Darkness tiptoed into the valley as street lights, car lights, house lights, and business lights greeted its silent return. As the birdsongs faded with the light, the crickets tuned up their fiddles and played for each other and for me.

In those twilight hours, I had some amazing conversations with God. But unlike Jesus, I seldom felt I *had* to pray. Though I might *say* I am nothing without God, I must think otherwise or I wouldn't allow the busyness of life to squeeze to the margins my time with him.

It's at this point the Jesus Experiment will stretch you and provide hope. Throughout the week, you may find it helpful to ask God to make you aware of your need for him. During the day, when you sense an emotional reluctance to pray, allow your feelings to remind you that you're not feeling and thinking about prayer like Jesus did. Remind yourself how desperately you need God's comfort, guidance, and strength, and ask him to make you always aware of your need.

> *Though I might* say *I am nothing without God, I must think otherwise or I wouldn't allow the busyness of life to squeeze to the margins my time with him.*

What did Jesus say and do?

As a boy, I didn't know much about prayer because I didn't grow up in a Christian family. I viewed God as a sort of heavenly Santa Claus—an old man with superpowers, who was there to fulfill my wishes. I would plead with God to help me pass a test, win a baseball game, or get a ten-speed bike for Christmas. Before eighth grade, I had never prayed with another person.

That changed when a friend asked me to join a group of Christian students for a prayer meeting. I don't remember why he asked, but I recall attending to impress a blue-eyed girl I thought would be there.

Because I had no idea what to say, I found a book of prayers and memorized a paragraph that seemed especially churchy. At least it sounded like the prayers I had heard the few times I had visited a church. I don't recall the entire prayer, but it started something like this: "Our most benevolent heavenly Father, we, Thy simple servants, beseech Thee, as the omnipotent sovereign over all creation, to hear our humble prayers." It was quite an impressive prayer, and even today I'm amazed I actually memorized the whole thing.

As the words left my lips, I opened my eyes a sliver to see how impressed my friends were with my eloquence. Especially the girl. My buddy caught me peeking and gave me a look that said, "What are you doing?"

I figured he was jealous. When he prayed, he didn't use words like *benevolent* or *omnipotent*. Nor did he use archaic English pronouns, such as *Thee* and *Thou*.

I left that short prayer meeting feeling impressed with myself; looking back, I realize my friends knew something about prayer I hadn't yet learned—genuine prayer sounds like children talking to their father.

> *I realize my friends knew something about prayer I hadn't yet learned—genuine prayer sounds like children talking to their father.*

Since then, I've studied many of the prayers of the Bible, especially those of Jesus. Though we know Jesus regularly found places of seclusion to talk with his Father, we don't know precisely what he said during his private times of prayer, apart from his prayer in Gethsemane. But that doesn't mean we have no idea what he said. From his public prayers, we gain insight into the kinds of things he prayed for when he was alone.

- He prayed with a heartfelt expression of thanksgiving (Matthew 11:25-27; John 11:41-42).

- He prayed for his friends and followers (John 17; Luke 22:32).
- He prayed for his enemies (Luke 23:34).
- He prayed for himself (Matthew 26:36-46).
- He prayed for guidance (John 5:20).
- He prayed that his Father would be honored (John 17).

What I say and do

These six topics of Jesus' public prayers provide an excellent guideline for our own prayers. I don't mean we should meaninglessly recite his words, like I sometimes do with the Lord's Prayer. Instead, we should personalize the topics as we talk with God.

For years, I've followed a similar pattern when praying. I've discovered that praying with a journal helps me stay focused. It also helps if I write the prayer and date it. I have a stack of prayer journals that serve as reminders of how God has answered past prayers.

If you don't have a prayer journal, I encourage you to start one. You can begin by writing a few words at the top of each page to remind you to pray like Jesus did.

> Thanksgiving to God
> Friends and family
> Enemies—problem people
> Myself
> Guidance
> God will be honored through me and others

Below each topic, jot down a few notes and a Bible verse. If you haven't been spending time alone with God each day, I encourage you to begin with five to ten minutes a day. Make it an amount of time that's significant but not intimidating. I've found it's easier to start small when building a habit and then expand once the habit is established.

I remember when Lance, the owner of the athletic club I mentioned in the first chapter, designed an ongoing workout regimen for me. He didn't say, "Bill, I want you to work out with Roger Miller." Roger was a competitive bodybuilder who trained at the gym. He could lift more weight than I could roll across the floor.

Nor did Lance team me up with David Oliphant, a cyclist who rode his bike ten thousand miles a year. My right knee was so bad it would have swelled to the size of a cantaloupe after the first twenty miles.

Instead, Lance gave me a fifteen-minute workout so short and easy I knew I would have fun doing it. Gradually, the amount of time and weight increased as I got stronger. The same is true with prayer. Prayer wasn't drudgery for Jesus, and it shouldn't be for us. If we start small and focus on consistent, steady growth, eventually we will come to see prayer as not only a meeting with God we desperately need, but also as a vital source of strength, wisdom, and direction in our lives. Like Jesus, we'll receive the wisdom and power we need to be like him and to deepen our relationship with God.

Like Jesus, we'll receive the wisdom and power we need to be like him and to deepen our relationship with God.

What's life changing about the Jesus Experiment is that you learn in a fresh way how to take what the Bible reveals about Jesus and apply it to your life. You don't just learn about Jesus, you develop a real-time connection with him. You're asking the necessary questions to discern how your feelings, thoughts, words, and deeds compare to his. By God's grace, in the process of seeking to abide in Jesus, you'll become more like him.

Now you must take the next step and put into practice what you've learned.

Living the Jesus Experiment

This Week

Throughout the day, ask yourself what Jesus would feel, think, say, and do at that precise moment, in the context of prayer. Now take note of your own responses. What are you feeling, thinking, saying, and doing? Ask God to make you more like Jesus.

Be sure to pause occasionally and remind yourself that the same resources available to Jesus are available to you as you abide in him. Keep asking God to enable you to see your need for him, so you'll seek him in prayer. This will soon become a self-regenerating process as you continually pray to learn how to pray. If you need help remembering to pause occasionally, find a way to build it into your daily schedule. For example, if you use Outlook, you can schedule a recurring "appointment" with a pop-up reminder. Or you might program it into your phone. If you're not a slave to electronic gadgets, or if your daily routine doesn't allow for such reminders, find a way to tie your "pauses" to regular events in your day, such as breaks, meals, activities, driving, etc. The point is to develop a sustainable habit that will help you in your quest to become more like Jesus.

Ask

Read John 5:19-20, 30 and John 17:20-21. On the chart on page 59, examine the left-hand column, noting what Jesus felt, thought, said, and did on the subject of prayer.

What does John 5:30 tell us about how Jesus viewed himself in relation to his heavenly Father?

_____

_____

_____

_____

How do you think that view affected his desire to spend time alone with God in prayer?

_____

_____

_____

_____

Observe

Think of a recent, specific situation in your life when you met with God alone and prayed. What motivated you to pray?

_____

_____

_____

_____

How have you been tricked into thinking prayer can be put off? Rate the following comments according to how strongly you agree or disagree.

1. "Work and other responsibilities are more important than time alone with God."

   (STRONGLY DISAGREE)   1   2   3   4   5   (STRONGLY AGREE)

2. "I don't want to bother God with the small stuff."

   (STRONGLY DISAGREE)   1   2   3   4   5   (STRONGLY AGREE)

3. "My life is going smoothly; I don't need to pray right now."

(STRONGLY DISAGREE)   1   2   3   4   5   (STRONGLY AGREE)

4. "I can make it on my own."

(STRONGLY DISAGREE)   1   2   3   4   5   (STRONGLY AGREE)

Fill in the center column of the chart (p. 59), recording what you feel, think, say, and do about prayer when you are self-reliant.

Evaluate

Prayerfully consider the benefits of private prayer. Ask God to bring to mind reasons why regular times of solitude and private prayer will benefit you and make you more like Jesus. Jot down whatever comes to mind.

_____

_____

_____

_____

How would abiding in Jesus produce a greater willingness to meet daily with God in prayer?

_____

_____

_____

_____

As you consider making prayer a part of your daily routine, describe your thoughts.

_____

_____

_____

How does a growing sense of your need for God prompt you to want to pray more?

_____

_____

_____

_____

Fill in the right-hand column of the chart, recording what you believe you would feel, think, say, and do about prayer if you were abiding in Jesus.

Apply

Prayer is simply talking with God. It doesn't require a large vocabulary, impressive thoughts, or incredible wisdom. It's a conversation between you and your heavenly Father. He's already seen and heard it all, so there's no need to try to impress him. Just tell him your feelings, thoughts, fears, and needs.

Here are some ideas to consider as you seek to live the Jesus Experiment.

- Buy a journal and jot down topics to guide your thoughts as you pray.
- Identify a time and place to meet alone with God. Start with an amount of time you know you can easily maintain—maybe five or ten minutes a day.
- Throughout the day, as you feel positive or negative emotions toward prayer, ask yourself what thinking triggered the emotion. Ask yourself what Jesus would have felt in that same situation. Take a moment and tell God you want to acknowledge your need for him and ask him to enable you to feel, think, speak, and act in private as Jesus did.

One Week Later

Record your thoughts about how God has worked in your life in the last seven days. How did abiding in Jesus and following his example in prayer make your life more rich and satisfying?

_____

_____

_____

_____

_____

_____

_____

_____

_____

_____

_____

_____

_____

_____

_____

_____

_____

_____

_____

_____

_____

_____

_____

_____

_____

_____

REGARDING PRAYER		
What did Jesus . . .	**What do I . . .**	
Feel? Though John doesn't mention how Jesus felt about prayer, it seems Jesus felt a need for the Father's strength and wisdom. Perhaps he felt a healthy sense of human inadequacy and his need for the Father.	*Feel when self-reliant?*	*Feel when abiding in Jesus?*
Think? Jesus considered himself unable to do anything without the Father. He thought his works were an expression of his heavenly Father, which must have motivated him to spend frequent time alone with God in prayer. (John 5:19-20, 30)	*Think when self-reliant?*	*Think when abiding in Jesus?*
Say? "I tell you the truth, the Son can do nothing by himself; he can do only what he sees his Father doing, because whatever the Father does the Son also does." (John 5:19)	*Say when self-reliant?*	*Say when abiding in Jesus?*
Do? Jesus' awareness of his need for his Father drove him to seek solitude where he could pray privately.	*Do when self-reliant?*	*Do when abiding in Jesus?*

Download full-size charts and study questions at www.jesusexperiment.com.

He Faced His Fears

AS I REVIEW MY LIFE, I believe fears have driven me as much as dreams. And it saddens me to realize they still do. I don't mean the sudden, reactive fear I felt recently when our burglar alarm went off at 3 a.m., launching me out of bed and down the stairs before I was fully awake. Or the moment of panic I felt when a plane I was flying in hit turbulence and bounced around like a pinball. Or when I was scuba diving with my wife off Santa Catalina Island in Panama and a down-current captured us, dragging us from 40 feet to 120 feet of depth in less than a minute.

That's the kind of fear that horror movies try to elicit. What I'm referring to is the gut-wrenching dread I battled when I heard my son had cancer. Or the apprehension I felt the day I quit my writing job and thought we could lose our home. I didn't just fear living on the street, I feared the humiliation of losing the respect of my family and friends.

It's no wonder fear affects me so profoundly. God hardwired our bodies to run or fight the moment we feel threatened.

One summer, my friend Jim Stewart and I were waterskiing on Lake Austin when our boat ran out of gas in front of a secluded house. Using our skis, we paddled the boat to the shore and tied it to a small dock. Had we been a bit smarter, or more experienced, we might have hesitated when we saw the sign posted on a light pole by the shoreline: PRIVATE PROPERTY. DANGER! KEEP OUT.

God hardwired our bodies to run or fight the moment we feel threatened.

What were we supposed to do? There wasn't another boat on the glassy lake, and cell phones wouldn't hit the market for another two decades. Shrugging our shoulders, we climbed out of the boat and stepped onto the dock. After looking around for any obvious signs of danger, we hurried across the blistering-hot wooden planks and over the prickly St. Augustine grass to the back of the ranch style house, then around to the front. As we walked under the carport, two Doberman pinschers, all snarls and teeth, raced around the corner of the house. I instantly understood the DANGER! part of the sign.

I froze as my racing heart pumped adrenaline through my body, my blood pressure spiked, butterflies fluttered in my stomach, my skin cooled with sweat, my face flushed, and my eyes focused. All my senses sharpened as I prepared to fight or flee. Of course, I learned all this later. I didn't conduct an on-the-spot check of my vitals.

What I did was think fast. Jim and I didn't discuss the best course of action. We didn't weigh the options. Instead, like terrified monkeys, we instinctively shimmied up the two poles supporting the carport roof, while the dogs snapped their jaws at our bare feet.

Alerted by her agitated pets, the owner, a middle-aged woman in a flower-covered apron, jeans, and a burnt-orange T-shirt, opened the back door and stepped out. When she saw us clinging to the poles, she asked with a Texas twang, "Why y'all teasin' them dogs?"

She stood with her hands on her hips, watching the dogs circle beneath us, waiting for an answer.

"We ain't teasin' 'em," I said with an equally Texan twang, all the while keeping my eyes on the Dobermans.

"Oh yeah, you're teasin' 'em," she insisted. "They figured you was gonna feed 'em, but you've climbed them poles so they can't get at ya."

Shaking her head, she started laughing. I relaxed when I realized she was an aspiring comic, not a homicidal homeowner who used dogs to do her dirty work. After patting the dogs on the head and praising them for their good work, she let them in the house. When we came down from the carport posts, she gave us enough fuel to get safely to a gas station.

In that situation, fear energized my body and enabled me to climb to safety. The problem we all face is that our bodies respond the same way to both real and *perceived* dangers.

The problem we all face is that our bodies respond the same way to both real and perceived dangers.

If we're fearful about our financial future, a loved one's health, giving a speech, or flying, our bodies prepare to fight or flee. When we obsess about such fears, it creates tremendous stress and can cause serious physical side effects, such as loss of sleep, headaches, diarrhea, sweating, rapid heartbeat, shortness of breath, and impotence. If not processed in a healthy way, fear can prevent us from taking risks, finding a job, finishing a project, or setting lofty goals.

Because fear enables us to successfully avoid or engage danger, it's essential we learn how to deal with it as Jesus did. On the night before his crucifixion, Jesus knew he would soon be betrayed, abandoned, rejected, tried, beaten, and crucified. He knew he would experience separation from his heavenly Father and suffer for the sins of mankind. No man could face such a day without fear.

The Jesus Experiment

What did Jesus feel?

Shortly before midnight, after eating the Passover meal, Jesus and his disciples sang a final hymn of praise and then hiked to the garden of Gethsemane. They passed through the deserted streets of Jerusalem, out the gate on the southeastern side of the city, and across the Kidron Valley to the foot of the Mount of Olives.

It's unlikely the disciples considered the walk to Gethsemane unusual, since Luke tells us that Jesus often went there (Luke 22:39). Once inside the garden, however, everything changed. Jesus left eight of the disciples at the gate and invited Peter, James, and John to follow him a little farther. Mark observes that Jesus "became deeply troubled and distressed" (Mark 14:33, NLT). Matthew tells us, "He began to be sorrowful and troubled. Then he said to them, 'My soul is overwhelmed with sorrow to the point of death. Stay here and keep watch with me'" (Matthew 26:37-38).

When Jesus entered Gethsemane, the reality of his impending death and temporary separation from his Father overwhelmed him.

Coming from anyone else, such a statement would seem exaggerated. And yet, when Jesus entered Gethsemane, the reality of his impending death and temporary separation from his Father overwhelmed him; he was like a man on death row facing not only execution, but also torture.

The word for "sorrow" in the original language of the Bible doesn't refer to sadness. Rather, it communicates the idea of being suddenly and surprisingly overwhelmed with terror, or the fear a child might experience upon being unexpectedly taken from home.[6]

Home, of course, is where Mom and Dad are, a place of safety and security.

It's hard to imagine exactly how Jesus felt because we don't have the same tight connection he had with God. I'm reminded of the day my wife and I were sitting on a bench at George Rogers Park near our home, watching our children play with other neighborhood kids. A toddler I didn't know was playing in the oversized sandbox with his heavy-duty, yellow Tonka dump truck, while his mother talked with a friend. The little boy used a plastic shovel to fill the back of the truck with sand, and then pushed it across the sandbox and energetically dumped the load. Every few minutes, he looked up at his mother, who smiled and praised his work.

After a while, the mother's friend packed up her belongings to leave. She must have needed help getting everything to the car, because the two women walked toward the parking lot. Unaware his mother had stepped away, the boy looked up after one of his dumping runs, expecting to see her. When she wasn't there, he stared for several seconds as if she might reappear—and then traces of fear began to pull at his lips, causing them to pucker. He swiveled his head from side to side, his saucer-sized eyes filled with concern. Then he stood, dropped his Tonka toy, and burst into tears. These were not the angry tears of a child whose mother refused a request for candy while grocery shopping. These were the tears of a child whose mother, for all he knew, had vanished from earth. His tears flowed from a horrible fear fed by a terrible loss.

Faced with the abandonment of his Father, Jesus dealt with a similar fear. Though anticipated, it was visceral and profoundly overwhelming.

That scene has always troubled me because it gave me a glimpse into the heart of an abandoned child. It's the kind of fear parents shelter their kids from. Faced with the abandonment of his Father,

Jesus dealt with a similar fear. Though anticipated, it was visceral and profoundly overwhelming.

Jesus felt afraid and alone, and the ordeal had only begun.

What did Jesus think?

Once in the garden, Jesus walked a short distance from Peter, James, and John. As he moved into the shadows of the gnarled trees, he knelt down and fell to the ground (Mark 14:35). The imagery is profound, because Gethsemane takes its name from an olive press that squeezes olives for oil. In a short time, his blood would be wrung from him as he suffered in the vise grip of agony.

Jesus moved far enough from his three friends to talk privately with his Father, but close enough to be heard. Though in the throes of agony, he knew it was important for his closest disciples to witness and learn from his travail. In Hebrews 5:7-8, we're told, "He offered up prayers and petitions with loud cries and tears to the one who could save him from death."

More than anything, he wanted to express despair and fear to his Father. He needed to connect with the only one who could stop the horrible chain of events.

What I feel and think

A couple of years ago, my son Paul and I went scuba diving off the coast of Bonaire. What makes this Caribbean island great is you can shore-dive along the entire leeward coastline. On our final dive of the trip, we decided to visit one of our favorite sites: Invisibles.

After we parked our white Toyota pickup close to shore, we donned our gear and waded into the water. Rather than surface swimming on our backs to get to the reef sooner, we descended right away, hoping to see an eagle ray feeding on the white sandy bottom.

The dive site is unique because it consists of two parallel reefs at varying depths. A couple of hundred yards offshore, the sandy bottom transitions into a reef that drops more than a hundred feet. Beyond the first reef, another sandy bottom stretches outward to a second, deeper reef, consisting of three underwater islands. The challenge is that the second reef can't be seen from the first, which is how the site got its name.

As we neared the first reef, several divers approached from the opposite direction. To avoid them, I swam away from the route I normally take. *Not a problem*, I thought, because I was familiar with the dive. In a few minutes, Paul and I had passed the first reef and entered an expanse of clear, blue water, knowing the second reef would soon appear.

But it didn't.

Several minutes later, Invisibles remained invisible. I signaled to Paul, and we swam deeper and further from shore in search of the second reef, which I knew would soon appear. A minute later, we couldn't see either reef.

Everything felt surreal. Wherever I looked, I saw royal blue. I had no sense of up or down, forward or backward or sideways. Blue surrounded me, like darkness shrouds a star.

Fear tightened my chest. I had heard stories about divers who had gotten disoriented in these waters, dove too deep, and disappeared. The only thing that checked my fear was a compass. I didn't know exactly where we were, but I knew where we had come from. In fact, I knew with absolute certainty because I had set the bearings on my compass before descending. Though we had diverged from the original route, I had followed the compass out, and I knew if I swam in the opposite direction, the compass would lead us to shore.

I had heard stories about divers who had gotten disoriented in these waters, dove too deep, and disappeared. The only thing that checked my fear was a compass.

That knowledge helped—somewhat. But swimming at depth,

in a world of blue, without a visual point of reference, infused me with fear, which sped up my heart, causing me to burn through my air supply. On our way to the safety of the shore, a huge hawksbill turtle swam so near that my son was able to pat him on the head. A short time later, we climbed out of the water to our waiting pickup.

I know my fear pales when compared to what Jesus suffered in Gethsemane. My experience, though, helps me understand what it's like to be lost in a dangerous place. I better understand why, as confusion and fear pressed upon Jesus, he entered the garden to talk with the only one who could give him direction. He needed his Father's guidance to get him though the night and the next day. He had to know he was headed down the right path.

We, too, must think of God when we're fearful. We must realize he alone can give us direction, just as my compass did in the Caribbean Sea. The moment fear whispers, whether the danger we face is real or perceived, we should remember that God will guide our steps through all peril.

What did Jesus say?

With his face pressed against the hard, dry earth, Jesus prayed, "My Father, if it is possible, may this cup be taken from me. Yet not as I will, but as you will" (Matthew 26:39).

Though considerable discussion in academic circles has centered on the contents of "the cup," it seems to me it contained the entire crucifixion event, from Christ's betrayal to his death.

The Passion of the Christ was a disturbing movie because it realistically portrayed the brutality Jesus suffered at the hands of the Romans. It showed how a flagellum—a short whip made of two or three leather thongs or ropes with small pieces of metal and bone attached at intervals—was used to shred Jesus' back and sides, exposing muscle and bone. It displayed the agony he suffered when a soldier pressed the crown of thorns into his scalp. It showed the

Week Four

cavalier cruelty of the Romans as they drove huge nails through his hands and feet into the wooden beams of the cross.

Because we've all experienced some level of physical pain, we shrink at such images. We understand why Jesus recoiled with fear as the hour approached. Yet I suspect his most tormenting thoughts and greatest fears centered not on the physical suffering he would endure, but on his impending abandonment by God the Father when Jesus' soul absorbed our sins. Not only would Jesus be absolutely alone for the first time in his life, but he would drink the sewage of every sinful thought, word, and deed of every person from Adam on down.

> *Because we've all experienced some level of physical pain, we understand why Jesus recoiled with fear as the hour approached.*

I have enough problems dealing with the guilt and shame of my own sins. Carrying the weight of the world's collective depravity is incomprehensible, like imagining infinity. Yet Jesus was fully aware he would bear it all.

No wonder he asked his Father if there was another solution that could redeem mankind. No wonder he prayed three times to have the cup removed. And no wonder he sweat blood—the internal torment and stress were so great they caused tiny capillaries to rupture, mixing blood with perspiration (Luke 22:44).[7] It was in Gethsemane that Jesus cried out to God and expressed both his fear of the cross and his desire to avoid it. It was also in Gethsemane that Jesus embraced the suffering of his life's mission.

What I say

Dr. Haddon Robinson, my preaching mentor in seminary, once said if he had seen Christ in Gethsemane, knowing what would happen the next day, he would have concluded Jesus would not endure the rigors of his trials and crucifixion.

Robinson's comment was insightful, but he brought it into focus when he noted that Jesus' real battle occurred in Gethsemane. That's where he faced his fears and settled the issue of the Cross. Once Jesus knew the Father's will, he never looked back. Upon leaving Gethsemane, Jesus shed no tears. He showed no fear. He walked with the strength and confidence of a man who knew he was in the epicenter of God's will.

Once we've discerned God's will and embraced the suffering it may bring, we've lifted our crosses and are following Jesus.

Jesus said, "If anyone would come after me, let him deny himself and take up his cross and follow me" (Matthew 16:24, ESV). I've heard numerous interpretations of these words. I believe we take up our crosses when we die to selfish desires and embrace God's pure desires. We take up our crosses when we enter a place of solitude and prayer and pour out our hearts to God. Once we've discerned his will and embraced the suffering it may bring, we've lifted our crosses and are following Jesus.

Each time you feel fear slipping its cold, shadowy fingers over your soul because you might lose something you value, pray, "Father, I desperately desire this relationship, job, or opportunity. But I want your will more."

We would all like to avoid the pain of losing money, our health, or a loved one, but we commit ourselves to following Jesus. When our wishes and his are in conflict, we must take up our crosses and follow him. We must choose his will and his wisdom over our own. As Jesus prayed in the garden of Gethsemane, "Not my will, but yours be done."

What did Jesus do?

We've already seen some of what Jesus did. He entered the garden and faced his fears in prayer. He expressed his desire to bypass the cross but submitted himself to his Father's will. What I mentioned only in passing was that he brought his three closest friends, Peter, James, and John, with him into Gethsemane.

Aware that death—dark, evil, and unstoppable—pursued Jesus, the exhausted disciples gave in to sorrow and drifted to sleep while the Lord agonized in prayer. Three times he lifted himself from the ground and approached his friends, only to find them sleeping (Luke 22:45). Their unwillingness to stay awake and pray, as Jesus had asked, demonstrates not only the frailty of well-intentioned friends, but the importance of not letting our emotions dictate our behavior.

> *Aware that death—dark, evil, and unstoppable—pursued Jesus, the exhausted disciples gave in to sorrow and drifted to sleep while the Lord agonized in prayer.*

It makes me wonder why the Lord brought these friends along. Did he hope they would alertly stand guard, like disciplined sentries? Or was he like a soldier who lets his young children sleep with him the night before a battle so they can cherish his presence for a short time? Or was their closeness a reminder for Jesus of what he was fighting for?

I don't know. But Jesus showed an understanding of their struggle. He told them, "The spirit is willing, but the body is weak!" (Matthew 26:41, NLT). I'm sure if the disciples had known Judas was on his way to the garden with a cohort of troops, they would have stood guard. Instead, their sorrow drove them to find solace in the quiet of sleep.

Jesus loved them nonetheless. On the night of his greatest fear, he wanted Peter, James, and John close enough to hear his cries—so close he could quickly reach them.

What I do

I think we all want and need someone close by when we're hurting. I know my wife and I do. It's fascinating that as I was writing this part of *The Jesus Experiment*, Cindy suffered a fear-inducing injury. My wife has been blessed with amazing health. In the decades I've known her, she has seldom been sick, never needed surgery—except for three C-sections—and stayed in excellent shape. For more than twenty years, she has danced several hours a morning, five days a week. She takes no medications and looks fifteen years younger than her age.

And then life happened. She suffered serious damage to the ligaments and muscles of her jaw when a dentist treated her mouth like the hood of a car. He left it open too long, slammed it around like a metal door, and dislodged the right disc. For a month, she could open her mouth only wide enough to slip in the tip of her little finger.

A couple of weeks after her injury, our friend Dr. James Yanney, a maxillofacial surgeon, joined us for dinner. His prognosis wasn't what either of us wanted to hear: Cindy would almost certainly need surgery . . . there was a 98 percent chance.

Not good.

He warned Cindy that after the operation she wouldn't be able to chew for six months.

"Your tongue will get strong," Jim said. "You'll have to eat small pieces of food and crush them against the palate of your mouth with your tongue."

"I've always wanted a strong tongue," she said with a smile. (Fortunately, her smile was unaffected.) "Can I dance?"

"No dancing," he said. "You can swim or ride a bike. But you can't do anything that moves your head up and down."

"Boring," she said. "Can I fly on a plane?"

"Maybe."

"Can I scuba dive?"

"Eventually," he said. "Well, maybe."

"That's the one sport Bill and I do together," she said, disappointed.

After Jim left, Cindy looked at me, and her brown eyes filled with tears. "I don't like this."

I wrapped my arms around her. "I'm sorry."

"Me too," she whispered. "I guess this is my cross."

"Appears that way," I said.

"I'm afraid I may never dance again. I'm afraid my face will sag and I'll look old."

"But you'll have a strong tongue," I said. "Maybe you'll win a strong-tongue competition."

She laughed. "I believe God brought this to me and intends to use it for good. It's given me a chance to talk with my friends at the gym about the Lord."

She paused a moment. "I would rather be in God's will with a bad jaw than outside his will with a good one." She said this matter-of-factly. I knew she meant it.

Her loss created fear in me. I feared she might suffer greatly, and that's not what I want for her. That concern drove us to God, where we acknowledged our fear and asked him to miraculously or medically heal her.

We prayed for the grace to abide in Jesus and embrace his will—even if it led down the path of suffering and loss. His will, not ours.

We asked him not to let her lose the joy of dancing. And then we prayed for the grace to abide in Jesus and embrace his will—even if it led down the path of suffering and loss. His will, not ours.

Fortunately, we were not alone. Cindy recruited her friends to pray for her, and I recruited mine.

It's amazing that this health crisis struck while we were studying how Jesus faced his fear in Gethsemane. It helped us look to the Lord and pray that we would process our fears as he did. We want to feel, think, speak, and act like him. Even if our greatest fears materialize, as they did for Jesus, we know for certain that God's will is a reliable compass in life's storms.[†]

Jeff's Story

Twelve years ago, one of my son's college friends, Jeff, lived with my family for a summer. He's a tall, wiry guy with a mellow disposition, a sharp sense of humor, and a soft heart toward God. During those three months, he became an older brother to Paul and a son to Cindy and me. He's now a thirty-three-year-old husband and father of a little boy.

Three months ago, Jeff's hopes and dreams collapsed when he was diagnosed with advanced melanoma, a fast-moving and lethal form of cancer. He and his family had to quickly and frantically leave their life and community in Colorado and travel to Houston, where Jeff underwent chemotherapy. He lost twenty pounds, his hair, and he suffered extreme bouts of nausea.

Staring into their greatest fear, Jeff and his wife had to embrace the likelihood that his life could end much sooner than they'd ever imagined.

Staring into their greatest fear, Jeff and his wife had to embrace the likelihood that his life could end much sooner than they'd ever imagined, leaving his wife a widow and his son fatherless. It's an understatement to say that embracing God's will proved challenging. There were many difficult nights spent crying out to God in tears, believing he had a purpose, and seeking peace in that knowledge.

And then the miraculous: The original diagnosis proved wrong. Instead, Jeff had sarcoma, a serious but less lethal form of cancer. Faced with the realization he had undergone unnecessary treatment,

---

[†]Three months after Cindy's injury, her jaw suddenly got better. She's now symptom-free.

yet also blessed with renewed prospects for a long and healthy life, Jeff and his wife soon had to embrace a new set of fears.

With the new diagnosis, Jeff will have to undergo a surgery that's only been tried on a handful of patients—a metal prosthetic pelvis replacement. He will likely be in a wheelchair for two years. But he should get better; he should live to see his son become a man.

As we recently talked late into the night, Jeff shared with me that, in the face of pain and despair, his friends have provided so much comfort. "My pain tells me I'm weak and of little value. The love of friends says I'm important. They care for me, and it gives me strength."

Each day as you encounter fear, whether fear of death, pain, financial loss, or something else, abide in Jesus and pray, "Not my will, but yours. Not my will for my future and the future of those I love, but yours."

And, like Jesus, draw friends close so their presence can strengthen you.

Living the Jesus Experiment

This Week

Every time you feel fear, ask yourself what Jesus would feel, think, say, and do in the same situation. What did he do in Gethsemane? Now take note of your own responses. What are you feeling, thinking, saying, and doing? As you abide in Jesus, ask God to enable you to respond more like the Lord, praying, "Father, not my will but yours be done."

Ask

Read Matthew 26:36-46 and Hebrews 5:7-10. On the chart on page 79, examine the left-hand column, noting what Jesus felt, thought, said, and did when faced with fear.

Contemplate the contents of "the cup" Jesus feared. How did prayer enable him to process his fear?

_____

_____

_____

_____

Observe

Think of a situation where you tend to be fearful when you're self-reliant and acting independently of God. Indicate the intensity of your fear of the situations below on a scale from 1–10, with 10 being the highest level of fear.

____ Failing a test
____ Losing a job
____ Death
____ Loss of a loved one
____ Personal injury
____ Public humiliation
____ Betrayal
____ Other (be specific) _____

Try to determine whether your fear is driven by a belief that you may lose someone or something you value. If so, who or what? On the lines below, in your journal, or on a separate piece of paper, briefly describe a recent situation in which you were fearful or an ongoing fear you experience.

_____

_____

_____

_____

_____

_____

_____

_____

Once you've identified a fearful situation, fill in the center column of the chart (p. 79), recording how you felt, thought, spoke, and acted in response to that fear.

Evaluate

Fill in the right-hand column of the chart, recording what you believe you would feel, think, say, and do in that same situation if you followed the example of Jesus and brought your fear to God in prayer, consciously releasing your fear each time you felt it.

Apply

Write down specific steps you'll take to prepare yourself for the next time you encounter fear. Spend a few minutes in prayer, asking God to guide you.

_____

_____

_____

Here are some ideas to get you started:

- On one side of a 3 × 5 card, write, "Not my will, but yours." On the other side, write, "Going a little farther, he fell with his face to the ground and prayed, 'My Father, if it is possible, may this cup be taken from me. Yet not as I will, but as you will'" (Matthew 26:39). Carry this card with you and review it throughout the day.

- Dedicate time to bring your fears to God and release them to him—acknowledging that you would rather be in his will and experience what you fear most than live outside his will. You could pray, "Father, please remove [note your specific fear] from my life. But even if you don't, I embrace your will."
- If you are obsessed about something you fear, try thinking about it for one minute and then releasing it to the Lord.
- Rehearse how you will respond the next time you encounter fear.
- Ask a close friend or family member to pray for you (or with you) in your area of fear.
- Make a commitment to ask yourself the next time you are fearful, "What would Jesus feel, think, say, and do in this situation?" Ask yourself, "How will my feelings, thoughts, words, and deeds be different if I abide in Christ and follow his example?"

One Week Later

Record your thoughts about how abiding in Christ and living the Jesus Experiment helped you trust God with your fears over the last seven days. How has abiding in Christ and following Jesus' example helped you find more confidence in the face of fear, and thus a more rich and satisfying life?

_____

_____

_____

_____

_____

_____

_____

_____

REGARDING FEAR		
What did Jesus . . .	**What do I . . .**	
Feel? Jesus felt grief and terror (Matthew 26:37-38)	*Feel when self-reliant?*	*Feel when abiding in Jesus?*
Think? Jesus thought he needed to express his desire to bypass the cross while at the same time expressing his submission to his Father's will. He wanted to be sure he was following the will of his Father. (Matthew 26:39)	*Think when self-reliant?*	*Think when abiding in Jesus?*
Say? "My Father, if it is possible, may this cup be taken away from me. Yet not as I will, but as you will." (Matthew 26:39)	*Say when self-reliant?*	*Say when abiding in Jesus?*
Do? Jesus went a short distance away from his friends, fell on his face, and prayed. He honestly expressed his fears and embraced God's will. (Matthew 26:36-39)	*Do when self-reliant?*	*Do when abiding in Jesus?*

Download full-size charts and study questions at www.jesusexperiment.com.

He Overcame Evil

THE FIRST TIME I remember struggling with temptation was as a five-year-old. A small church was under construction across the street from our house. One morning, I wandered over and saw a carpenter using a flashlight to look around a storage room. I had never seen a handheld light before and decided I needed one.

I ran back to my house and asked my mother to buy me a flashlight. When she refused, I begged. When that didn't work, I whined. When that didn't work, I cried. After all my parental manipulation tools failed, an idea dawned. I would take the money from her purse and ask the carpenter to buy the flashlight for me. I knew this was wrong, but I didn't care. So I stole a dollar, gave it to the carpenter, and he bought me the coveted tool.

I feared my mother would notice the missing cash, but she didn't.

She did, however, notice my new flashlight. How could she miss it? I was an inexperienced thief and made no effort to hide my prize.

Curious, she asked where I had gotten it. I told her a carpenter working across the street had given it to me. I figured that would end her inquiry and I would spend the rest of my life playing in the dark crawl space under our house. Instead, she grabbed my hand and walked me to the church. There she spotted the carpenter hammering a nail into a stud.

"Did you give this to my son?" she asked in her sweet Southern drawl, holding up the flashlight.

I felt mortal fear as my life teetered on the high-wire of his response.

The carpenter looked at the flashlight and then at me. "Yes, ma'am, I sure did," he said with a wink only I could see.

I couldn't believe my luck. He'd told a lie to protect me. In less than one day, I had stolen, lied, and become part of a conspiracy. Dark stains appeared on my not-so-innocent soul.

In less than one day, I had stolen, lied, and become part of a conspiracy. Dark stains appeared on my not-so-innocent soul.

Looking back, I realize I wasn't equipped as a five-year-old to resist the urge to lie and steal. Unfortunately, neither are adults. All we have to do is reflect on our thoughts and actions over the last twenty-four hours to make this abundantly and embarrassingly clear. It's not that we're all criminals; we're not. But we often treat evil as a friend rather than a mortal enemy.

The truth is, we're wired from birth to seek gratification apart from God.

We partner, sometimes unwittingly, with evil spiritual forces that use temptation as a magnet, pulling the iron of our base appetites to the surface of our minds, urging us to act without God.

Like all sin, my childhood theft began with a thought and grew into a plan. Although I've gotten older, bigger, and wiser, one thing hasn't changed: The battle between good and evil is fought in the private chambers of my mind.

Most people don't have a strategy for resisting evil, though it's everywhere. It flashes from computer screens, enticing us to enjoy illicit sex. It whispers from grocery shelves, begging us to indulge a sweet tooth. Evil drives us to acquire power for selfish ends and convinces us to cling to wrongs we've suffered until bitterness grows into a rage that leaks sarcasm or explodes into verbal and physical shrapnel. Evil hammers us with self-loathing, driving us to addiction, depression, or even suicide. Submitting to evil causes us to minimize wrong, justify evil, and lie about our sin.

Evil is ever-present, all around us, tempting us throughout the day, every day. We're most susceptible to temptation when experiencing an emotional or physical extreme, such as euphoria, exhaustion, depression, or despair. When we're up, we justify evil as a reward. When we're down, we use it to medicate our pain. The good news is our struggle shows we're alive. The bad news is that we'll have to fight it as long as we live or surrender to its rule. I don't know about you, but I refuse to raise the white flag.

Some people think temptation is inherently evil. It's not. Temptation is simply an enticement to do evil. For Jesus, the Spirit of God led him into the wilderness to be tempted by the devil (Matthew 4:1; Mark 1:12). This occurred after his baptism in the Jordan River by his cousin, John

> *We're most susceptible to temptation when experiencing an emotional or physical extreme, such as euphoria, exhaustion, depression, or despair.*

the Baptist. As Jesus dripped with water, the crowd of onlookers heard a voice from heaven declare, "This is my Son, whom I love; with him I am well pleased" (Matthew 3:17). Such a public affirmation from God must have awed those present and filled Jesus with confidence. With his Father's approval, he had officially launched his public ministry.

After this high point, the Spirit directed Jesus into the wilderness and guided him through a forty-day fast and repeated temptations. I suspect Jesus felt euphoria as he left the Jordan River and hiked into the desert. But as the days slowly passed, single file, he would have become increasingly exhausted, both physically and emotionally. In this context, Jesus faced repeated temptations.

Test Me, Lord

Decades ago, while working on summer staff at Campus Crusade's international headquarters in Arrowhead Springs, California, I learned to walk with Christ, talk about my faith, and disciple young men. One night toward the end of the summer, I sat on a grassy slope on the southern edge of the San Bernardino Mountains, looking at the valley below. With twinkling stars overhead and shimmering lights below, I prayed, "Lord, test me when I get back to college. I'm ready."

With twinkling stars overhead and shimmering lights below, I prayed, "Lord, test me when I get back to college. I'm ready."

Within a month, I learned how unprepared I was for what followed. My dream of reuniting with my ex-girlfriend hit a snag when she rejected my attempt to start over. I don't blame her. I had hurt her deeply, and she viewed my newfound faith with skepticism. At just that time, a friend who worked with me at an upscale restaurant offered me a "de-edger." He promised the drug would replace my pain with a pleasant buzz. Disappointed with God, I gave it a try. That single act launched me on a downward spiral that ended a year later with a drug-induced psychotic break. Fifteen years had passed since I'd stolen the dollar from my mother's purse. I had come to faith in Jesus and started growing. Yet I was no better prepared to resist temptation than I had been as a boy.

That horrifying incident convinced me that evil exists and the evil one wants to destroy me. I've never again asked God to test me. Nor have I taken satanic attacks lightly.

I don't believe Satan personally assaulted me—he's neither omnipotent nor omniscient, and I wouldn't warrant his direct attention. But he is dangerous. As Peter warns, "Your enemy the devil prowls around like a roaring lion looking for someone to devour" (1 Peter 5:8).

Though the devil doesn't possess divine attributes, he has a massive army of fallen angels, or demons, who carry out his plans.

Though the devil doesn't possess divine attributes, he has a massive army of fallen angels, or demons, who carry out his plans (Revelation 12:4).[8] Such truth might be unnerving if the evil one and his cohorts could read our minds, but they can't. At least the Bible doesn't say they possess such powers. With millenniums of observation and experience, though, they don't need to mind read. As *The Screwtape Letters* by C. S. Lewis illustrates, demons know human weakness and how to trip us up.

Satan must have thought Jesus would be vulnerable to similar temptations. And though the Lord may have been subjected to scores of temptations over the forty days, he only told his disciples about three.

Temptation One: Gratifying a Legitimate Need in an Illegitimate Way

The first temptation was straightforward: The devil told Jesus, "If you are the Son of God, tell this stone to become bread" (Luke 4:3). The question implied Jesus might *not* be the Son of God. It prodded him to prove his identity and satisfy his hunger by performing a miracle.

There's nothing wrong with eating bread when you're hungry. And it wouldn't have been wrong for Jesus to turn stones into bread and eat them—unless in doing so he acted independently of his Father. That's what Satan wanted Jesus to do: stop abiding in his Father by exercising his own divine power to meet a need. Similarly, he wants us to stop abiding in Christ by independently meeting our physical need for food, clothing, shelter, sex, love, and companionship.

> *That's what Satan wanted Jesus to do: stop abiding in his Father by exercising his own divine power to meet a need.*

"My wife is seriously ill"

It's easy to justify meeting a legitimate need illegitimately. A few years ago, a man approached me after I had spoken at a men's conference. After telling me his wife had been seriously ill for several years, he said, "We haven't had sex in ages. I've been viewing porn on the Internet and figured it was okay, since my wife can't meet my needs."

I expressed sympathy for his wife and concern for his situation. Then I asked, "Do you think God would approve of what you're doing?"

"I'm not sure," he said. "That's why I asked you."

I reminded him that Jesus said, "Anyone who looks at a woman lustfully has already committed adultery with her in his heart" (Matthew 5:28).

"They're not flesh-and-blood women," he said. "They're just pictures."

"But they're pictures of real women," I said. "Do you think you're minimizing the wrong of what you're doing?"

"I'm not sure."

"If you have a valid need that's not being met by God, does that mean you should disregard his command and meet that need yourself?"

He gazed at his shoes for a moment and then looked up. "I see what you mean."

It's understandable how a man in his situation could rationalize acting apart from God; but in doing so, he stumbled into a world of sin, propped up by lies.

Food fills a hole

After writing a book on secret addictive behaviors, I got a heart-breaking letter from a young woman whose love affair with food had destroyed her sense of self-respect. Though she wasn't overweight—in fact, she had little body fat and worked as a model—she used carbs to fill her need for love.

Meeting our needs in destructive ways is inappropriate because it forces us to stop abiding in Christ and act independently of God.

"Unlike men, food is always there," she wrote. "It demands nothing in return. It never puts me down. It gives me peace, at least for a while."

Certainly needing love, affection, food, or sex is appropriate. But meeting those needs in destructive ways is inappropriate because it forces us to stop abiding in Christ and act independently of God.

Resist the lust of the flesh by depending on God

Jesus made it clear that our need to obey God's Word is greater than our physical needs.

Jesus told the tempter, "It is written: 'Man does not live on bread alone, but on every word that comes from the mouth of God'" (Matthew 4:4). In other words, although Jesus could have met his physical needs apart from God, it was more important to do it God's way.

I believe the apostle John, one of the Lord's closest disciples, was commenting on the temptation of Jesus when he said, "Do not love the world or anything in the world. If anyone loves the world, the love of the Father is not in him. For everything in the world—the cravings of sinful man, the lust of his eyes and the boasting of what he has and does—comes not from the Father but from the world" (1 John 2:15-16).

The "world" to which John refers is any system that leaves out God. The three worldly cravings he noted parallel the three temptations of Jesus. The "lust of the flesh" refers to our human appetites that seek gratification in ungodly ways. I think John meant that when we seek to satisfy these appetites inappropriately, it's not the Father acting through us—he has no desire for evil and would never seek it through us. Because Jesus never acted independently of the Father, he resisted the devil's temptation by staying aligned with God and his Word.

Temptation Two: Asking God to Serve Me

The year I prayed for an hour a day proved to be one of the most painful of my life. I suffered burnout from working full time as a pastor, leading my family, speaking at men's events around the country, and writing a daily devotional for an international ministry. In six years, I wrote the equivalent of twenty 250-page books, plus a sermon a week.

Fearing a moral and emotional meltdown, I quit my writing job. Though that removed one weight, the fear of financial ruin hung over me like an executioner's blade. The shadow of despair, black as ink and cold as death, seeped out of my pain and pulled me into its dark lair. Though I never considered suicide, I repeatedly asked God to take my life. Not only did he refuse to reward my devotion to prayer and hard work with an expanded ministry, he wouldn't even end my suffering by killing me—preferably during sleep or in some other painless way.

That agonizing experience taught me something I'd known all along: God is not obligated to serve me; I'm obligated to serve him.

I believe Jesus' second temptation pivoted on this truth. Because Jesus had already said he would only meet his needs according to God's plan and provision, Satan asked him to prove his faith:

That agonizing experience taught me something I'd known all along God is not obligated to serve me; I'm obligated to serve him.

> *Then the devil took him to the holy city and had him stand on the highest point of the temple. "If you are the Son of God," he said, "throw yourself down. For it is written: 'He will command his angels concerning you, and they will lift you up in their hands, so that you will not strike your foot against a stone.'" (Matthew 4:5-6)*

Quoting Psalm 91:11-12, Satan challenged Jesus to prove his unflinching faith in God's promise to rescue him. By leaping from the Temple, not only would Jesus demonstrate his faith, he would dazzle the crowd below like a trapeze artist who performs aerial stunts without the aid of bars, ropes, or a safety net. The entire nation would quickly recognize him as the promised Messiah. He could move from the Jordan River to the wilderness to the throne of God's kingdom in less than two months. And he could bypass the suffering of the Cross.

The devil wanted Jesus to test God by forcing a supernatural rescue. But Jesus' purpose was to do the will of the Father who sent him (John 5:30), not to force the Father to do the Son's will—or, even worse, Satan's will.

That's why Jesus said, "It is also written: 'Do not put the Lord your God to the test'" (Matthew 4:7). In other words, "Don't do something to manipulate God into doing what he has no intention of doing. Don't say or do something that you think will pressure God into serving you." That was the sin committed by the ancient Israelites when they demanded God prove his presence by giving them water in the wilderness (Deuteronomy 6:16). By referring to that event, Jesus corrected Satan's distortion of Scripture and resisted the second temptation.

If God would obey our commands, or bow to our manipulations, we could wow the world and win instant acclaim.

Resist the pride of life by submitting to God's will

Had Jesus jumped from the Temple, he would have embodied what the apostle John refers to as "the pride of life"—that is, arrogance or worldly boasting about what someone has or does (1 John 2:16, NASB). Though we'd all like to be recognized for our accomplishments, no accomplishment would be greater than figuring out how to control God. Such power would transform us into something greater than a superhero. If God would obey our commands, or bow to our manipulations, we could wow the world and win instant acclaim. We would be greater than any lion tamer or fighter pilot. We would have the power of God at our fingertips. We could do or have anything.

At the opposite end of the spectrum from such delusions of grandeur—but no less manipulative—we have a tendency to think God will repay us for our sacrificial, noble, or spiritual acts. After becoming a Christian, I thought my devotion to God would obligate him to bring back my girlfriend. It didn't. Years later, when I prayed an hour a day for a year, my desire was genuinely to know God better. But I also had a distorted, hidden belief that my devotion somehow obligated God to grow my ministry. It didn't.

No one has power over God. When we try to manipulate him to do something that will dazzle our friends or even fulfill our deepest longings, we carry out the plans of the evil one—even if the dazzling deed would accomplish great good. God isn't like a food server with whom we place an order for a marriage partner, better job, successful surgery, or any other request and expect he will rush to heaven and quickly bring it back to us. As we saw in the previous chapter, Jesus didn't demand anything from the Father; he submitted to his will.

> *The Jesus Experiment is challenging because it helps us come to terms with the fact that Jesus never considered using his Father's power to serve himself.*

The Jesus Experiment is challenging because it helps us come to terms with the fact that Jesus never considered using his Father's power to serve himself. Instead, he prayed to discern the Father's will and carry it out. Jesus' miracles resulted from the Father working *through* him, not *for* him.

Temptation Three: Seizing Control

Several years ago, Paul Allen, one of Microsoft's founders, moored his majestic yacht—the *Octopus*—along the Columbia River in Portland. This massive ship dwarfed every other boat on the waterfront.

Curious, I googled the ship's name and quickly discovered that the world's eleventh largest super yacht has "two helipads on the top deck (one in front and one on the back, each with a helicopter), a sixty-three-foot tender docked in the transom, seven boats, a pool on one of the upper decks, a basketball court, and two submarines."9 Make no mistake about it: one of the world's richest men doesn't boat down when he sails the seas.

The beauty of the *Octopus* mesmerized me. The more I read

about it, the more I wanted it. I wanted to sail the seven seas with my family and friends, scuba dive the reefs of the world, and feast on delicious food prepared by a French chef and served in the ship's wood-paneled dining room. If the boat were mine, the world would envy me as much as I envied Paul Allen.

Of course, Paul Allen's wealth so exceeds mine that I don't envy him as much as I envy those who possess something just beyond my reach . . . something like a better car, a nice home, a flashier entertainment system, a bigger ministry, a wider circle of influence, or something else I don't have and can't acquire.

Resist the lust of the eyes by worshiping and serving God alone

The apostle John refers to such worldly cravings as "the lust of the eyes" (1 John 2:16). It's the desire to seize something that's not mine. Because all men and women have a soft spot for stuff that glitters, Satan assumed Jesus would too. He also believed Jesus would pay a fair price to get it. And he offered him much more than a measly yacht.

Because all men and women have a soft spot for stuff that glitters, Satan assumed Jesus would too.

Satan took Jesus to the summit of a mountain and in an instant showed him the kingdoms of the world and their splendor. "'All this I will give you,' he said, 'If you will bow down and worship me'" (Matthew 4:8-9).

These were the most impressive kingdoms of the ancient world—and Jesus could have it all. He could be lord of an empire greater than that of Alexander the Great or Julius Caesar. He could rule the *entire* world.

Though Satan is not omniscient, he knows Scripture well enough to realize the Messiah would one day rule the kingdom of God. He also knew the path to that kingdom would involve rejection, suffering, and death. Satan offered Jesus immediate control of a worldwide kingdom, a shortcut to avoid the pain. There was only one small catch: Jesus would have to bow down and worship the father of lies.

I suspect Satan tried to make it sound like a low price to pay. After all, they were in a secluded place. No one would observe or record it. What's one act of worship in exchange for lordship over the entire planet? But the offer was loaded with more hatred and crime than Hitler or Stalin could command. Jesus replied, "Away from me, Satan! For it is written: 'Worship the Lord your God, and serve him only'" (Matthew 4:10).

Jesus quoted Deuteronomy 6:13 and added the phrase, "and serve him only." He knew that an act of worship would make him subservient to the devil. The bowing might be momentary, but the service would be forever.

Had Jesus bowed to Satan, he would have abided with the evil one, not his Father. He would have seized control of a kingdom rather than waiting for the Father to give him a more glorious one.

I think most people would admit they don't desire material possessions as much as the message they send—I'm in control of my life; I've subdued the marketplace and it serves me; I'm god of my own world. Status and stuff demand others bow to our wisdom and power.

When we move away from God and seize control of something we want, we serve the evil one and carry out his plan, not God's.

When we move away from God and seize control of something we want, we serve the evil one and carry out his plan, not God's. Jesus immediately resisted that temptation, and we must too. We must abide in Jesus, worshiping and serving God alone, while we wait for him to provide what will enable us to fulfill his plan for our lives.

The Jesus Experiment

Before the temptations in the wilderness, Jesus lived to know and serve his Father. That's why he was able to cast aside Satan's enticements decisively. Like an art critic who can spot a forged masterpiece because he studied the original, Jesus immediately saw the evil of Satan's tactics. The better and more intimately we know God, the easier it is for us to identify and overcome evil in our lives.

What did Jesus feel and think?

Though Jesus likely felt everything from euphoria to exhaustion during his forty days in the wilderness, his thinking remained clear. In each of the three temptations, he saw beyond the bait to the underlying trap. Though famished, he didn't see rocks turned to bread as food to satisfy his appetite and prevent starvation. He knew Satan was asking him to meet a legitimate need in an illegitimate way—apart from the Father. He didn't see a leap from the Temple as a way to prove God's faithfulness to him. He saw the evil one tempting him to put his own needs above God's will. And he didn't see the kingdoms of the world as a desirable, immediate goal. He saw Satan tempting him to shortcut God's timetable by seizing an evil kingdom rather than waiting for God's perfect kingdom. Jesus knew that the devil was seeking his subservience, not urging him to worship and serve his Father.

Jesus knew that the devil was seeking his subservience, not urging him to worship and serve his Father.

What I feel and think

Our emotions bounce around during the course of a day, week, month, or year. Decades of research and counseling others on compulsive and addictive behaviors have taught me we're most vulnerable to temptation when experiencing mood swings—high or low. Of course, that doesn't mean temptation can't trip us at any time.

A few years ago, a woman who struggled with a shopping compulsion sat in my office. Her normally bright blue eyes looked dull as she gazed out the window at snow-covered Mt. Hood in the distance.

"I blew it," Sue said. "I told myself I could return the purse without buying anything else. I really believed I could do it this time. But when I got to the store, I saw that it was the week of the yearly women's sale. So I started looking around. Not to buy anything, of course; just to see the deals."

"And—?" I prompted.

Sue exhaled. "I walked out of the store three hours later, carrying four bags and more than two thousand dollars in credit card receipts."

"What did John say?"

"I didn't want to tell him, so I planned to let him find out when he got the credit card bill. But when I got home, he was waiting at the door. We had a horrible fight. He insisted I return everything, which I did."

As we talked, I handed her a card on which I had written the three kinds of temptations Jesus faced.

> *Are you tempted to meet a legitimate need in an illegitimate way?* This covers a lot of temptations: sexual needs, financial needs, food needs, and relational needs.

> *Are you tempted to test God by asking him to serve you, rather than seeking to serve him?* We often deceive ourselves into believing God is obligated to reward our devotion. Our prayers sometimes indicate our desire for God to serve our purposes. When we're tempted,

we need to be alert to this trap and continually submit to God's will.

Are you tempted to seize control from God rather than waiting for his provision? Are you seeking to get something your eyes want rather than waiting for God to provide for you? If so, you may be worshiping or serving something or someone other than God.

Sue looked over the card for a moment. "The third one," she said emphatically. "That's me. When I see something I want, especially clothing or accessories, I feel an urge to buy it. I don't give God a thought. I hate to say it, but clothing becomes my god."

While identifying the temptation she most often faced didn't provide Sue with the insight needed to resist, it did expose the spiritual root of her temptation—the desire to seize control from God. Until we are able to honestly identify our areas of temptation, we will be helpless to resist their alluring siren songs.

Until we are able to honestly identify our areas of temptation, we will be helpless to resist their alluring siren songs.

What did Jesus say and do?

I'm impressed by how quickly and concisely Jesus dealt with temptation. He didn't toy with the tempter, like a cat with a mouse. He immediately saw through Satan's deception and distortion of Scripture and rebuffed him with biblical truth. Jesus' words and actions indicate a clear alignment with his Father and a steadfast refusal to do anything that might hurt that bond.

What I say and do

As Sue and I continued talking, I told her how understanding and breaking the four-step temptation cycle would help her follow the example of Jesus.[10]

The first step involves *preoccupation*—thinking about the sinful act. During this stage, we fill our minds with memories that prepare us to give in to the temptation. The more we fantasize about the deed, the more excited we become to pursue it.

I asked Sue if she was aware of the sale before returning the purse.

"I saw an advertisement the weekend before," she admitted. "But I figured I could return the purse, maybe look around for a few minutes, and leave without purchasing anything."

I explained that, by going to the store, she entered the second stage of the temptation cycle—*ritualization*, which involves a seemingly harmless act, or trigger, that precedes acting out. For instance, a person with an eating compulsion might ritualize by grocery shopping on an empty stomach. A person with a sexual compulsion might ritualize by surfing the Internet without a filter or accountability. And a shopping addict would return a purse during a sale.

It's crucial to break the cycle before it reaches this stage because once we ritualize, we'll almost always take the next two steps: *acting out* and *shame*. We commit the act and then feel guilty about it—that is, until the next time we're tempted to repeat the cycle.

To avoid reaching the first stage of the temptation cycle, we have to abide in Christ by meditating on biblical truth, as Jesus did.

To avoid reaching the first stage of the temptation cycle, we have to abide in Christ by meditating on biblical truth, as Jesus did. This will enable us to keep our minds focused on our love for Jesus and not on the object of temptation.

Because our minds can't focus on more than one thing at a time, it's wise to focus on what is good. As Paul advises in Philippians 4:8-9, "Whatever is true, whatever is noble, whatever is right, whatever is pure, whatever is lovely, whatever is admirable—if anything is excellent or praiseworthy—think about such things. Whatever you have learned or received or heard from me, or seen in me—put it into practice. And the God of peace will be with you."

"To break temptation at the second stage," I told Sue, "we need to remember that Jesus urged us to be as shrewd as snakes and innocent as doves. This means taking steps to avoid rituals or triggers that lead us down the temptation cycle."

"How do I do that?" she asked.

"We have to know our habits and tendencies. The key is to identify and remove every act that triggers a sinful desire. For you, that might mean getting off certain mailing lists or avoiding newspaper ads."

Sue nodded her head. "You're right. And probably cutting my credit cards and getting on a cash-only budget—which John has been telling me for months."

"And don't forget," I said, "Scripture is the most powerful weapon against the enemy. Memorize passages that encourage you and return your focus to Jesus."

Though we may not always be able to control our desires, we can control the opportunities by getting rid of triggers.

Toward the end of our meeting, I reminded Sue that every temptation is an attempt by Satan to get us to rely on ourselves, rather than God, to meet a need. Everything else is a cloak behind which he hides that single fact.

As Sue left my office that afternoon, I knew she had a difficult path ahead. But I also knew she could successfully resist temptation if she would meditate on Scripture and remove all triggers from her surroundings.

We all need to meditate on passages of Scripture that strengthen our minds and help us focus on abiding in Christ, not satisfying our base desires by giving in to temptation. We also must identify every ritual that precedes acting out sinfully and ruthlessly remove it from our lives.

By urging us to pray, "Father, lead us not into temptation," I think Jesus meant we should ask God never to allow us to encounter an opportunity to sin when we have a desire to sin.

If desire and opportunity intersect, there is a strong likelihood we will sin. Though we may not always be able to control our desires, we can control the opportunities by getting rid of triggers.

Living this stage of the Jesus Experiment should force us to think past the temptation to the evil spirit behind it. It should also give us a specific strategy for resisting temptation as Jesus did. We need to remember that the evil one wants to use us, just as God does. I vote for God.

Living the Jesus Experiment

This Week

When tempted this week, pause and ask what Jesus would feel, think, say, and do in the same situation. Now take note of your own responses. What are you feeling, thinking, saying, and doing? As you abide in Christ, pray God will help you respond to temptation as Jesus would.

Ask

Read Matthew 3:16-17; 4:1-11. On the chart on page 103, examine the left-hand column, noting what Jesus felt, thought, said, and did when he encountered Satan's temptation.

How do you think Jesus felt at his baptism, before entering the wilderness? Why?

_____

_____

_____

_____

Observe

Make a list of situations in which you struggle with the same temptations Jesus faced: meeting a legitimate need in an illegitimate way, asking God to serve you, seizing control from God.

_____

_____

_____

_____

1. Which of the following legitimate needs do I try to meet illegitimately?

   ____ Housing
   ____ Food
   ____ Finances
   ____ Acceptance
   ____ Clothing
   ____ Sex
   ____ Recreation
   ____ Other (be specific) _____

2. How do I ask God to serve me?

   ____ Praying he will serve my purposes
   ____ Bargaining with him

_____ Trying to force him to serve me by taking unwise risks

_____ Expecting him to reward my devotion by giving me what I want

_____ Asking him to deliver me from a mess I've created

3. Am I trying to seize control from God? If so, how?

_____ Walking away from God because of disappointment

_____ Pursuing my agenda without God

_____ Serving something or someone besides God

_____ Choosing to live by my own moral values instead of God's

_____ Coveting or buying something I don't need or can't afford

Think of a specific recent temptation you've experienced in one of those three areas. Briefly describe the temptation below.

_____

_____

_____

_____

_____

_____

_____

Fill in the center column of the chart on page 103, recording how you felt, thought, spoke, and acted in response to that temptation.

Evaluate

Fill in the right-hand column of the chart, recording what you believe you would feel, think, say, and do in that same situation if you were abiding in Christ and successfully resisted the temptation.

Apply

Review your list of temptations from the Observe step and identify your area of greatest vulnerability. What steps can you take to more consistently resist this temptation by depending on Christ? Put a check by the strategies that will help you the most, and take those steps over the next week.

    ____ Figure out why this is tempting to you

    ____ Talk about it with a friend or pastor

    ____ Memorize a Bible verse that addresses the issue

    ____ Get an accountability partner

    ____ Identify what triggers the temptation and remove it from your life

    ____ Each time you think of the temptation, mentally walk though the Jesus Experiment

    ____ Other (be specific) _____

One Week Later

Record your thoughts about how living the Jesus Experiment helped you trust God when you were tempted over the last seven days. How has abiding in Christ and following his example helped you resist temptation as you pursue a more rich and satisfying life?

REGARDING TEMPTATION		
What did Jesus . . .	**What do I . . .**	
Feel? The Bible doesn't say what Jesus felt in the wilderness. But since the temptations came after his baptism, he may have felt at first optimistic. Later he likely felt emotionally and physically drained. (Matthew 3:13—4:11)	*Feel when self-reliant?*	*Feel when abiding in Jesus?*
Think? Jesus quickly saw through the lies by comparing what the devil said to the truth of the Old Testament. (Matthew 4:3-10)	*Think when self-reliant?*	*Think when abiding in Jesus?*
Say? Jesus quoted from the Old Testament and exposed how Satan had distorted the Scriptures. (Matthew 4:4, 7, 10)	*Say when self-reliant?*	*Say when abiding in Jesus?*
Do? Jesus was led by the Spirit into the wilderness where he fasted and prayed for forty days. He then encountered the devil and resisted Satan's temptations. (Matthew 4:1-11)	*Do when self-reliant?*	*Do when abiding in Jesus?*

Download full-size charts and study questions at www.jesusexperiment.com.

What Jesus Did in Public

He Stuck to His Mission

THE OUTDOOR SURVIVALIST on television sported a stubby beard, worn jeans, a faded camo shirt, and dirty hiking boots. Holding a small magnifying glass he had swiveled out of a vinyl case and speaking from the corner of his mouth, he said, "If you're ever stranded in the elements overnight and need to start a fire, this is an essential tool."

After watching him demonstrate on a self-made bird's nest of kindling, I felt inspired. I grabbed the magnifying glass from my desk drawer, retrieved a section of the newspaper, and walked onto our front porch where the fall sun sent soothing, warm light through the nippy air.

I folded the newspaper, placed it on the porch, and waited. The sun's light hit the paper, but nothing happened. I waited a bit longer—still nothing. I bent down and touched the paper. It felt cool.

Then I held the magnifying glass between the sun and the paper, focusing a few inches of sunlight into a beam that formed a bright spot on the paper. Almost instantly, gray smoke curled up from the white dot.

When I recall this exercise, I'm reminded of the power of focused light. Water is the same way. Steam rising from a teakettle is unfocused and puffs harmlessly into the surrounding air. But directed steam surging through a turbine generates electricity.

When we channel our mental, emotional, and physical energy into a single purpose, we possess great power.

What's true of light and water is also true of people. We've all seen the difference when we focus on a topic we're studying or a task we're performing. When we channel our mental, emotional, and physical energy into a single purpose, we possess great power.

Unfortunately, we don't normally live like this. We tend to live unfocused lives, and our strength diffuses like sunlight or dissipates like unharnessed steam.

That's why knowing our mission is so crucial. It's our mission that explains why we exist and what we hope to achieve. It reveals what we value.

You can identify your mission by answering three questions:

- What is my purpose for being alive?
- How am I uniquely equipped to fulfill that purpose?
- What do I value above all else?

After his resurrection, Jesus told his disciples, "As the Father has sent me, I am sending you" (John 20:21). That should help you answer the first question. And, as we'll soon see, the Lord's mission was to seek and save the lost (Luke 19:10). As believers, that's our mission as well.

Yet we also need to recognize that each person is gifted differently to fulfill that mission. So, for example, my personal mission might look very different from yours. In writing a personal mission statement, be sure it uniquely expresses how you believe God will use you to help others know and love Christ.

What unique talents will help you fulfill your purpose? Mine include writing, speaking, and developing friendships. Are you artistic? Are you talented at working behind the scenes to make things happen? Are you a good listener or counselor? Are you able to take a vision and develop a strategy to bring it to reality? Are you gifted as a teacher? Are you athletic? These are the types of questions that will help you identify your unique talents to fulfill your purpose as a follower of Christ.

In writing a personal mission statement, be sure it uniquely expresses how you believe God will use you to help others know and love Christ.

Next, you need to determine what you value that will shape your mission statement. For example, I value God and family. I also value other people and their opinions, and I seek to interact with them in nonthreatening and intelligent ways. Perhaps you value spending time with people of other races or socioeconomic backgrounds. Maybe you enjoy hospitality, caring for the elderly, or providing relief for the suffering. It could be you value truth, music, fun, children, or a host of other things.

Once I knew my unique talents and values, I was able to write my mission statement: *My mission is to know God, and in his power, use my communication skills, resources, and relationships to help others know Christ and grow in him.*

Because I'm especially passionate about rescuing orphans in India and challenging and equipping men, I've concentrated my life on those two areas of work. The point is, once you identify your mission, you must find outlets to act. If you're passionate about homelessness, get involved in a shelter. If your heart breaks when you hear about kids growing up without a mom or dad, get involved in a mentoring program. Identifying your mission reveals what you value—what you're passionate about—and is necessary to focusing your life.

Identifying your mission reveals what you value—what you're passionate about—and is necessary to focusing your life.

I've shown you my mission statement and how I arrived at it, so you'll understand what I mean when I say that Jesus stuck to his mission. It may help you figure out your own mission, if you haven't already. Of course, identifying your mission and sticking to it are two different things. The rest of the chapter will explain how to stay focused on your mission.

The Mission and Divine Appointments

If ever a man was primed for a conversation with Jesus, it was Zacchaeus, whose name in Hebrew means "pure" or "righteous." I'm sure his neighbors found his name ironic—like calling a drug dealer "Doctor," or a bank robber "Reverend." As a *chief* tax collector in ancient Israel, Zacchaeus and his underlings taxed fellow Jews, paid the Romans, and skimmed enough to make themselves rich. Zacchaeus was anything but *pure* or *righteous*.

The tax collector

So hated were tax collectors that religious leaders spoke of them in the same breath as "sinners"—prostitutes, murderers, and thieves. When Jesus came to town, an unpopular and short man like Zacchaeus wouldn't be able to see over the crowd or squeeze through it without risking an elbow to the face.

Not easily dissuaded, Zacchaeus raced ahead of the throng and climbed a sycamore fig tree—a good choice because it has low-hanging branches that even a short man could reach. Perhaps the branch extended over the road, since Jesus had no trouble spotting the town's most despised citizen sitting in the catbird seat.

Though we don't know for sure why Zacchaeus was so determined to see Jesus, I have a good idea. Before Jesus arrived in Jericho, Zacchaeus may have heard a few stories about encounters Jesus had earlier in the day.

In one story, Jesus exposed a Pharisee and praised a tax collector. Both men entered the Temple to pray. The Pharisee prayed aloud, thanking God he wasn't like "other men—robbers, evildoers, adulterers—or even like this tax collector" (Luke 18:11). Meanwhile, the tax collector stood far away and beat his breast, praying, "God, have mercy on me, a sinner" (Luke 18:13). Jesus concluded the story by saying the tax collector, not the Pharisee, returned home justified before God.

The rich man

Later in the day, Jesus told a rich young ruler to keep all the commandments if he wanted to inherit eternal life. The man, with cast-iron confidence, assured Jesus he had kept each one from his youth. In other words, he believed he loved God above all else and his neighbor as himself. But Jesus, in order to help the man realize he might not love his neighbor quite as much as he loved himself, told him to sell all he had and give it to the poor (Luke 18:22). No doubt stunned, and certainly saddened, the rich man walked away chastened and exposed.

> *Just as the Pharisee in Jesus' parable trusted in his own righteousness to win God's favor, the rich man trusted in his wealth.*

Just as the Pharisee in Jesus' parable trusted in his own righteousness to win God's favor, the rich man trusted in his wealth. Had Jesus praised him for his righteous life and simply asked for a donation, the young man might have complied. But Jesus askd for *everything*—not just a token offering, but everything in which the man trusted. For the young ruler, this was too much to ask.

The blind man

Shortly after that encounter, a blind man pleaded with Jesus to show mercy and heal his eyes. But this wasn't a silent plea, with a bow and lacing of the hands. This man shouted at the top of his lungs. The leaders of the procession, annoyed by the distraction, ordered him to be quiet. Instead, he yelled even louder. When Jesus came along, he stopped, had the blind man brought to him, and asked what he wanted.

"Lord, I want to receive my sight."

Jesus responded, "Receive your sight; your faith has healed you" (Luke 18:42).

Zacchaeus wanted to see Jesus

After these earlier encounters, Jesus entered Jericho, Zacchaeus's hometown. I believe Zacchaeus had heard that Jesus praised the humility of a tax collector over the arrogance of a Pharisee. If so, I suspect it gave him hope. I think he heard that Jesus exposed a rich man's greed and misplaced faith. If so, it likely pierced his conscience. I suspect he heard that Jesus healed a man because of his faith. If so, maybe, just maybe, it meant God would accept him, too. If so, each word stoked Zacchaeus's spirit and fueled his determination to see Jesus.

Keep in mind that Jesus didn't get up in the morning, gather his disciples, and set the agenda for the day:

9:00 a.m.: Tell the story about the Pharisee and tax collector.

10:00 a.m.: Talk with the rich, young ruler.

11:00 a.m.: Heal a blind man.

11:30 a.m.: Call down Zacchaeus, a notorious tax collector, from the limb of a tree.

Noon: Eat lunch with Zacchaeus at his home.

Neither did Jesus tap into his divine nature to get an advance peek at the morning. Though his Father told him about certain future events, such as his death and resurrection, there is no indication he told Jesus everything. Yet Jesus knew God had orchestrated the events of his day so he could fulfill his mission—just as he does for us.

Because Jesus always abided in his Father, he walked by faith every moment of the day, just as we will when we abide in Jesus. God prepared Zacchaeus's heart for an encounter with Jesus, as he prepares the hearts of people we meet. And just as Jesus knew that God ordered his daily events to best accomplish his mission, we must know that God organizes our lives to most effectively fulfill our mission.

Don't miss this profound truth: God arranges our schedules so our lives will have maximum impact. This

> *"We are God's workmanship, created in Christ Jesus to do good works, which God prepared in advance for us to do."*

is what the apostle Paul meant when he said, "We are God's workmanship, created in Christ Jesus to do good works, which God prepared in advance for us to do" (Ephesians 2:10).

This is important to realize because it's easy to think we're somehow different from Jesus in this regard—that he knew exactly how God planned every moment of his life. He didn't. We must listen for God's guidance in order to learn how to carry out his will in our lives.

As Zacchaeus sat on the tree branch, his legs dangling, he not only wanted to *see* who Jesus was, but he was ready to *hear* what he had to say (Luke 19:3-6). Once he heard and saw, he was ready to *do* the good work that God set before him (Luke 19:8).

Truth Seekers and Resisters

While in college, I worked as a waiter at a restaurant in Austin. One day, a young woman about my age joined the service team. Mary had shoulder-length black hair, hazel eyes, and a smile that made the world a better place. Over the course of several months, I found out she wanted to learn how to read the Bible.

So Cindy and I invited her to our apartment for dinner.

After the meal, the three of us sat on the couch, with Mary in the middle. I opened my Bible to the story of the prodigal son and handed it to Mary. She placed it in her lap and caressed the pages as she might the face of a child. Then, at my request, she began reading aloud—slowly, as if savoring every word like a chocolate éclair.

As the story progressed, I noticed her fighting back tears. Toward the end, when she read about the son returning and his father accepting him, she began to cry softly. Shaking her head from side to side, she regained her composure and her radiant smile appeared.

"I can understand it. I can understand it," she whispered. "I was always told I couldn't understand it. But I can."

According to conventional wisdom at the time, no godly Jew would knowingly associate with a tax collector, much less enter his home to share a meal.

When I remember Mary, I think of Zacchaeus. Both had been searching for truth. Both had been told they couldn't get close to God. And both were found by Jesus.

Upon seeing Zacchaeus, Jesus told him to come down immediately, because "I must stay at your house today" (Luke 19:5). Jesus didn't ask for an invitation. He said he *must* stay with Zacchaeus. So compelling was his mission, and so strong his faith that God ordered his day, that he felt confident thrusting himself into Zacchaeus's life.

Looking Past Critics

Immediately, Jesus faced resistance—not from the tax collector, but from everyone else. When he went to Zacchaeus's house, we're told, "all the people saw this and began to mutter, 'He has gone to be the guest of a "sinner"'" (Luke 19:7). According to conventional wisdom at the time, no godly Jew would knowingly associate with a tax collector, much less enter his home to share a meal. They believed such an act would defile their soul like salmonella on a sandwich.

This is where we have a cultural disconnect. Nowadays, most people don't think in terms of "sinners" or "spiritual defilement." In fact, in our society people who ignore social, economic, religious, and race barriers to connect with unsavory characters might end up on the cover of *People* magazine.

When Jesus invited himself to Zacchaeus's house, the people believed it meant Jesus wasn't a prophet because prophets condemned sin, they didn't associate with it.

When Jesus invited himself to Zacchaeus's house, the people believed it meant Jesus wasn't a prophet because prophets *condemned* sin, they didn't associate with it. Even worse, it meant Jesus was a sinner himself. He could have eaten with anyone in Jericho, yet he chose to eat with a low-life tax collector. Not only that, he invited himself. Such disregard for societal standards offended the crowd like a broken sewer line.

A gentleman's club

While speaking on the East Coast a few months ago, I met a surgeon who heads the surgical department at a hospital in the Midwest.

He got my attention when he said, "Many Christians think it's wrong for men to visit a gentleman's club. You know, a nude dance bar."

Wanting to hear more, I hid my surprise. "What do you think?"

"I think it's perfectly fine," he said. "I'm a devout Christian, and I often go to a gentlemen's club with my friends. I hardly even notice the girls anymore."

I asked if his vision was okay. He laughed and said it was 20/20.

"What do you think?" he asked.

I paused a moment, considering how to answer. Finally I said, "All the healthy men I know who have visited a strip club have told me it messed up their minds and hurt their marriages. Jesus said a man commits adultery in his heart by looking lustfully at a woman who isn't his wife."

"But I don't look at them lustfully," he insisted.

"What does your wife think of these visits?"

He paused, smiled, and said, "She doesn't know, of course."

The ancient Jews felt as strongly about Jesus eating with a tax collector as I did about my new acquaintance visiting a "gentlemen's club."

The analogy isn't perfect because Jesus wouldn't visit a gentleman's club if he were here today, any more than he visited a brothel in first-century Palestine. But I could see him having lunch with the owner of the strip club, a dancer, or one of the customers.

> *Jesus wasn't concerned with offending the Pharisees, and he wouldn't be concerned today about offending religious leaders.*

Jesus wasn't concerned with offending the Pharisees, and he wouldn't be concerned today about offending religious leaders. In fact, throughout his ministry, he refused to allow opponents to shape his actions. He consistently looked past his critics to his mission. They would soon discover why he was willing to eat with a tax collector.

But first, Zacchaeus made a shocking statement—a statement that demonstrated why he so passionately wanted to see Jesus.

"Look, Lord! Here and now I give half of my possessions to the poor, and if I have cheated anybody out of anything, I will pay back four times the amount" (Luke 19:8). Zacchaeus's generosity greatly exceeded the demands of the Old Testament law, which required full restitution plus 20 percent (Leviticus 6:1-5). The tax collector had voluntarily upped the standard as an act of gratitude.

After witnessing this dramatic conversion and announcing that salvation had come to Zacchaeus and his family, Jesus enthusiastically declared his purpose: "For the Son of Man came to seek and to save what was lost" (Luke 19:10).

I can't help but wonder why, in one day, Jesus told the parable of the Pharisee and the tax collector, talked with the rich young ruler, healed the blind man, and invited himself to Zacchaeus's house to eat. I think he did it for a single reason—the same reason he did what he did every day—to fulfill his mission.

As he did for Jesus, God divinely sets our steps. And like Jesus, we need to act based on an awareness that God has prepared our day to most effectively accomplish our mission.

Jesus Stuck to His Mission

The Lord's mission was "to seek and to save the lost." And he allowed nothing to distract him from accomplishing it.

Time and again, Jesus reminded his disciples about his mission—which was also *their* mission and *ours*. On the day he called his first disciples, they were casting a net into a lake. He told them, "Come, follow me. . . . I will make you fishers of men" (Matthew 4:19).

Time and again, Jesus reminded his disciples about his mission— which was also their *mission and* ours.

After violating all cultural mores and speaking with a Samaritan woman at a well, Jesus told his disciples, "Open your eyes and look at the fields! They are ripe for harvest" (John 4:35).

Jesus often used vivid illustrations to instruct his followers about their mission. He spoke of sowing the seed of the word of God into men's hearts (Luke 8:1-12), and he called his disciples to let their light shine before others (Matthew 5:14-16).

Ignoring Distractions

Because I work from home, I continually deal with distractions. Remember the pecking blue jays? Unread e-mails, football scores to check, news to read, phone calls to answer, phone calls to make, my wife asking for help, the dog wanting to go out, the dog wanting to come in, the dog wanting to eat, the dog wanting to play ball, the doorbell ringing, mail to sort. The list goes on and on.

When I have a rapidly approaching deadline and the work is piling up, do the distractions stop? Do they peek in my office, see me hard at work, and slip away as quietly as a sunset? No way. It's my responsibility to tune them out and focus on my work. When I do, I'm better able to fulfill my mission.

Imagine what Jesus' life would have looked like if he had allowed himself to get distracted by every religious debate, disappointed follower, unhappy family member, and misunderstanding.

Imagine what Jesus' life would have looked like if he had allowed himself to get distracted by every religious debate, disappointed follower, unhappy family member, and misunderstanding. He would have spent all of his time running from one crisis to another.

But Jesus never allowed distractions to divert him. One day he visited two sisters, Martha and Mary. After Jesus arrived at their home, Martha continued to hustle around the kitchen, preparing a meal fit for a king. Meanwhile, Mary sat on the living room floor, listening to Jesus.

Angered that Mary wasn't helping, Martha confronted Jesus. "Don't you care that my sister has left me to do the work by myself? Tell her to help me!" (Luke 10:40).

I find it amusing that Martha had the gall to rebuke Jesus and tell him what to do. Instead of ordering Mary to help her sister, though, Jesus said something we all need to hear: "You are worried and upset about many things, but only one thing is needed. Mary has chosen what is better, and it will not be taken away from her" (Luke 10:41-42).

In that home, with those two women, Jesus modeled how to avoid distractions. While praising Mary for enjoying his presence instead of busying herself with less important matters, he also resisted Martha's attempt to pull him away from what he considered more important.

The Jesus Experiment

Thus far we've seen Jesus

- lock onto his mission
- look past his critics
- recognize God's ordering of events in his life
- take bold action to accomplish his mission (We'll look at this more in the next chapter.)
- not allow distractions to prevent him from doing God's work

Had the Lord's mission been to win the favor of Jericho's citizens, he wouldn't have eaten with Zacchaeus. Had his mission been to please the Pharisees, he wouldn't have healed a crippled man on the Sabbath. Had his mission been to please Peter, he wouldn't have gone to Jerusalem to die. Had his mission been to please his mother and brothers—they said he was "out of his mind" and insisted he leave with them (Mark 3:21)—he would have abandoned the crowd he was teaching. Had his mission been to appease Martha, he would have sent Mary into the kitchen.

Changing the trajectory of our lives because of critics who don't share our mission is like an airline pilot taking directions from a passenger.

Changing the trajectory of our lives because of critics who don't share our mission is like an airline pilot taking directions from a passenger. We cannot allow critics to hijack our lives and destroy our mission.

By sticking to his mission, Jesus knew he would be misunderstood, misrepresented, resented, resisted, rejected, and ultimately killed. If he'd listened to his critics and followed their advice, he might have had fewer enemies. But he wouldn't have realized his purpose.

What did Jesus feel and think?

In the pursuit of his mission, Jesus felt a range of emotions:

- Anger (Mark 3:1-5)
- Compassion (Matthew 9:36)
- Fear (Mark 14:33)[11]
- Joy (John 15:11)
- Love (John 19:26)
- Peace (John 14:27)
- Sorrow (Matthew 26:37)

Jesus' mission served as a magnifying glass, focusing his mind so he could listen to his emotions but not allow them to direct his actions. He saw his purpose for what it was: the most important mission in human history. That reality shaped his every thought. His mission was like the magnetic north pole to a compass, guiding his thinking in every situation, even when his dark emotions might have pulled him away, as we saw when he prayed in Gethsemane.

What I feel and think

Before I knew Jesus, I believed God was real but couldn't be known, so nothing mattered. After I became a Christ follower, I knew that God was real and nothing *else* mattered.

My life was so radically changed by Christ that knowing him better and helping others know him seemed like the only work worth doing. That mission propelled me forward—to seminary, preaching, and writing. But sometimes my sense of purpose runs out of steam, loses momentum, and rolls to a stop.

When that happens, we go from a life of *purpose* to a *purposeless* life. We no longer focus all our thoughts, words, and actions on a singular mission. We merely do the job. We become like the basketball player who, when asked what he was doing, said, "Practicing my shot." That's not how we should want to view our lives. We should be like the player who answered the same question by saying, "I'm training to win a championship."

> *My life was so radically changed by Christ that knowing him better and helping others know him seemed like the only work worth doing.*

Regardless of what we may *feel* at any given moment—glad, sad, mad, or bad—we must stay focused on our mission. For me, when research and writing prove tough or tedious, I have to remember I'm not simply writing a book, I'm seeking to know God better and provide a resource to help men and women know Christ and grow in him.

What did Jesus say and do?

I remember reading a story about a child who feverishly worked on a drawing during his preschool class. Curious as to what had captured his attention, the teacher approached his desk, leaned over, and gazed at the image.

"What are you drawing?"

"A picture of God," the boy said without looking up.

"But nobody knows what God looks like," the teacher said matter-of-factly.

"They will when I'm done."

I admire the kid's confidence, but the truth is, he won't capture God on a piece of paper any more than he could catch moonbeams in a jar. I suspect the boy's image of God would look strangely like himself and the sum of his experiences—as would ours. God is so far beyond us that we could no more see him than we could see the back of the sun. And I can't even see the back of my eyes.

As God in the flesh, Jesus' mission was to show us what God is like and how we should live our lives.

This reality makes the claim of Jesus even more amazing. He once told his disciple Philip, "Anyone who has seen me has seen the Father" (John 14:9). As God in the flesh, Jesus' mission was to show us what God is like and how we should live our lives. His words and works illustrated how God seeks out people who desperately need him. Every word he uttered and every act he performed contributed to the fulfillment of the mission his Father had given him.

What I say and do

Flying home to Portland several years ago, I got in a conversation with a fellow traveler. He told me about a struggle he was having in his marriage. After hearing his story, I told him how Jesus had helped my wife and me through some tough times.

Over the next three hours, he listened intently and asked a lot of questions. Before the plane landed, he said he wanted forgiveness from his past mistakes. He said he needed hope that his marriage could get better. Though he didn't embrace faith in Jesus, he took a step closer.

What happened at church the next Sunday took me by surprise. No, I didn't see the man from the plane. Instead, a woman whose husband had recently started attending church approached me between services.

"My husband was sitting behind you on the flight from Dallas," she said.

"Really?" I asked. "I didn't see him. Where was he sitting?"

"Directly behind you." She paused, contemplating what to say next. "He didn't want you to see him."

"Why not?"

"Because he wanted to watch you, to see how you would treat the man beside you. He's suspicious of Christians and wondered if your faith was real."

"And—?" I asked slowly, not immediately recalling the details of the conversation.

"And, Bill, how you talked to that guy and what you said . . . it helped."

I take plenty of flights on which I'm so tired that I sleep from takeoff until initial descent. On other flights, I avoid conversations. But on that particular flight, God placed searching men beside me and behind me. And because I was *As you pursue your mission, God will focus his life through you like sunlight through a magnifying glass.* acting with an awareness of God's ordering of events to best fulfill my mission, he gave my words a focus and power they wouldn't otherwise have had.

I'm usually cautious, and even hesitant, to engage in a spiritual discussion with strangers. At such times, I find it helps to ask myself, "Why am I here? Why has God placed this person in my life?"

As you pursue your mission, God will focus his life through you like sunlight through a magnifying glass. It's likely you'll encounter critics as you pursue your mission. Don't let them sidetrack you. Distractions will tap-tap-tap, seeking to redirect your attention. Shoo them away, ignore them, or move to a location where they can't get to you. But don't let them drain valuable time. Instead, recognize that God is directing your steps and boldly seize the opportunities he brings your way as you abide in Christ.

Living the Jesus Experiment

This Week

As you pursue your mission, ask yourself, what did Jesus feel, think, say, and do about his mission? Now take note of your own responses. What are you feeling, thinking, saying, and doing about your mission? As you abide in Christ, pray that God will enable you to live with a constant awareness that he is ordering your daily life in order to best fulfill your mission, just as he did with Jesus.

Ask

Read Luke 18:9–19:10. On the chart on page 129, examine the left-hand column, noting what Jesus felt, thought, said, and did about his mission.

How does Jesus describe his mission (Luke 19:10)?

_____

_____

_____

_____

_____

How does Jesus demonstrate his focus on his mission in this passage?

_____

_____

_____

_____

_____

What are some potential distractions for Jesus?

_____

_____

_____

_____

Observe

Reflect on Jesus' mission and the commissioning of his followers in Matthew 28:19-20. How would you define their mission?

_____

_____

_____

_____

Our mission is our purpose for being here that reflects what we value most. With that idea in mind, write a brief description of your mission. Remember that, as believers, we all have a common purpose (John 20:21; Luke 19:10), but as individuals, we each have a unique mission that will help us accomplish that purpose.

My mission is to . . .

_____

_____

_____

_____

How has God uniquely equipped you to fulfill your purpose?

_____

_____

_____

_____

_____

_____

Briefly describe a recent, specific situation in your life when you were distracted from your mission because of self-reliance.

_____

_____

_____

_____

_____

_____

What are the most powerful distractions from your mission? Check those that apply, and add your own.

   __ Critics
   __ Family conflict
   __ Misunderstanding
   __ Unimportant details
   __ Other opportunities
   __ Other (be specific) _____

Fill in the center column of the chart (p. 129), recording what you feel, think, say, and do about your mission when you are self-reliant.

Evaluate

Fill in the right-hand column of the chart, recording what you believe you would feel, think, say, and do if you abided in Jesus, living with an awareness that God ordered your life in order to best fulfill your mission.

Apply

Develop a plan to prepare yourself for the next time you're distracted from your mission. Spend a few minutes in prayer, asking God to guide you.

_____

_____

_____

_____

_____

Here are a few ideas to get you started:

- Write specific steps you will take to help accomplish your mission. For example, if part of your unique mission includes painting or singing, what will you do to develop your talent and paint or sing more often?
- Discuss your mission and potential distractions with a friend or small group. Ask someone to hold you accountable for staying on mission.
- Meditate on a verse that helps you remember the importance of being focused on your mission in Christ (e.g., Luke 19:10; Matthew 28:19-20; Colossians 1:28-29).
- Rehearse how you'll respond to distractions in the future.
- Place a reminder of your mission on a frequently viewed surface, such as a mirror or computer screen.

One Week Later

Record your thoughts about how living the Jesus Experiment helped you stay focused on your mission and abide in Christ over the last seven days. How has this enabled you to live a more fulfilling life?

_____

_____

_____

_____

_____

_____

_____

_____

_____

_____

_____

_____

_____

_____

_____

_____

_____

_____

_____

_____

_____

_____

_____

_____

_____

REGARDING MISSION		
What did Jesus . . .	**What do I . . .**	
Feel? Jesus may have felt compassion for Zacchaeus because of the rejection he suffered and joy because of his spiritual interest.	*Feel when self-reliant?*	*Feel when abiding in Jesus?*
Think? Jesus may have been thinking he needed to meet the man who showed such interest in him that he climbed a tree to see him. Jesus likely saw Zacchaeus as a man ready to embrace the Kingdom of God.	*Think when self-reliant?*	*Think when abiding in Jesus?*
Say? "Zacchaeus, come down immediately. I must stay at your house today." (Luke 19:5) "Today salvation has come to this house." (Luke 19:9) "The Son of Man came to seek and save what was lost." (Luke 19:10)	*Say when self-reliant?*	*Say when abiding in Jesus?*
Do? He looked up at Zacchaeus and called him. (Luke 19:5) He went to Zacchaeus's house. (Luke 19:6) He listened and responded to Zacchaeus's commitment. (Luke 19:9)	*Do when self-reliant?*	*Do when abiding in Jesus?*

Download full-size charts and study questions at www.jesusexperiment.com.

He Took Action

I ONLY REMEMBER a single word from a disquieting experience I had while in college. I don't remember where I was, or the season or year. The speaker's name and face have faded from memory, and the subject about which he was lecturing has slipped my mind.

What I recall is fighting to keep my eyes open as the speaker droned on—until he diverted onto a topic that captured my attention like the day a fighter jet streaked low over my house in Roswell, cracking the sound barrier.

That single-word topic?

Procrastination.

At that time, I was putting off so many things in my life that the single word, like a surgeon's scalpel, cut open my soul and exposed my fears. Fears such as flunking out of college because I had put off reading, studying, and writing papers—I was so far behind that just thinking about it still causes me stress. Fears such as losing my spiritual edge because I kept deferring prayer and studying God's Word.

Looking back, I think Gloria Pitzer described my life as a twenty-two-year-old when she wrote:

Procrastination is my sin.
It brings me naught but sorrow.
I know that I should stop it.
In fact, I will—tomorrow."[12]

Or as Mark Twain reportedly said, "Never put off till tomorrow what you can do the day after tomorrow."

I imagine you know how it feels. Perhaps you've put off something important—and then suddenly and unexpectedly, like death, the due date arrived and you weren't ready. This was the feeling I lived with every day.

That speaker's digression brought me face-to-face with my tendency to procrastinate.

Confronted, I was now motivated, and I began an intensive examination of Proverbs. I figured Solomon, of all people, would have much to say about procrastination. I was wrong. In fact, I was relieved to discover the word isn't in the Bible. As I continued my study, though, I found a different word.

Sluggard.

Images of slimy slugs came to mind, slow-moving, lazy creatures that only come out at night. When I looked in the dictionary, it defined a sluggard as "a habitually lazy person."[13] I put down the dictionary and returned to Proverbs. The more I read, the more I saw the word, and the more I felt convicted. After spotting the word *sluggard* fourteen times in Proverbs, I knew it described me perfectly when I procrastinated.

Here are some of the more glaring characteristics of a sluggard/procrastinator:

> Doesn't like to start things and refuses to take action.
> Doesn't like to finish things.
> Doesn't like to face things.
> Rationalizes, creating excuses to justify laziness.
> Is dishonest about the core of the problem, blaming it on other people or circumstances instead of facing the truth and taking responsibility.

I don't like to think I'm lazy. I mean, that list doesn't describe the kind of person I want to be. But I daily battle the lure of laziness. Well, that's not always true. Sometimes there is no battle. On those days, Laziness and I kick back and relax—like old pals, characters in a movie, best friends. Sometimes we hang out for days at a time, going on adventures like watching TV, devouring a novel, or sitting in my office reading the news.

We tend to embrace things we enjoy and delay things we dislike, even if we know they must be done.

I've found most people squirm when the subject of procrastination comes up. I suspect it's because we're all guilty of it. We tend to embrace things we enjoy and delay things we dislike, even if we know they must be done. They could be things that require discipline—like working, losing weight, or replacing a bad habit with a good one.

I can't imagine Jesus hanging out with Laziness any more than I could imagine my wife smoking a cigar. Jesus associated with tax gatherers and sinners, but there's no way he allowed Procrastination, that master time-thief, to erode his incentive or steal strategic opportunities God had prepared for him.

Though I'm sure Jesus relaxed and recharged his emotional

batteries, I'm also convinced he never put off until the next day what needed to be done right away. Nor did he delay difficult tasks, or dealing with difficult people, because he had other, less important but more enjoyable things to do.

The night before his crucifixion, Jesus told his Father, "I have brought you glory on earth by completing the work you gave me to do" (John 17:4).

The night before his crucifixion, Jesus told his Father, "I have brought you glory on earth by completing the work you gave me to do."

Pause for a moment and consider that statement. It's amazing, isn't it? Wouldn't you like to say that about your life someday? I know I would.

As we saw in the previous chapter, Jesus knew his mission and, living with a constant awareness that God ordered his life to best accomplish it, he stuck with it. Seeking to accomplish his Father's will, he received his daily marching orders and carried them out appropriately and on time. Because he refused to procrastinate, he seized every opportunity the Father sent his way.

A Man Born Blind

Occasionally, people ask me tough questions. For instance, why do good people suffer while evil people prosper? Why did my mother, father, sibling, or friend die young? Why did my son or daughter suffer that disease or injury? Why did I lose my job when I did everything right? Why did he or she break up with me when I was certain we would one day get married?

I try to answer in a gracious and intelligent way, but some questions defy a logical answer. I think that's why, when the disciples saw a beggar who was born blind, they asked Jesus, "Rabbi, who sinned, this man or his parents, that he was born blind?" (John 9:2). Though their question might sound insensitive, it was based on their understanding of Scripture. God had told the Israelites that he punished children for their father's sins, to the third and fourth generation (Exodus 20:5).[†] If that were all God had said on the subject, they could have justifiably concluded the man's blindness was caused by the sins of his parents. But the issue wasn't so simple. God also said children are *not* punished for the sins of their parents, but for their own sins (Ezekiel 18:19-22).

Thinking they knew the only possible answers, the disciples asked their question. But Jesus gave a third answer, one they had not considered: "'Neither this man nor his parents sinned,' said Jesus, 'but this happened so that the works of God might be displayed in his life'" (John 9:3).

Jesus didn't mean the man or his parents had never sinned. Everyone sins. He meant the man's blindness wasn't punishment for sin. Rather, the man had endured a lifetime of darkness so God's power could be displayed through the removal of his blindness.

The man had endured a lifetime of darkness so God's power could be displayed through the removal of his blindness.

It's as if Jesus had shown the disciples the box top to a five-thousand-piece puzzle. The man's life would soon make sense. There would be meaning to the opaque pieces of the puzzle, the years of suffering. All the heartache he and his parents had endured would soon be worth it. All the ridicule and rejection he had endured would be redeemed. All the questions, all the doubt, all the hurt had been permitted by God for a divine purpose.

The blind man didn't schedule an appointment with Jesus the way you or I would do with a doctor, nor was it merely a "lucky" encounter. It couldn't have happened by chance. Jesus said the man had been born blind with *this moment* in mind.

[†] I take Exodus 20:5 to mean, not that the sins are literally passed from one generation to another, but that the evil behavioral bents of a father would be passed to his children as he raised them.

But what about the blind man and the years that led up to the moment of his healing? As a boy, how often did he ask his parents, "Why did God make me blind?"

And how often did his parents say, "Son, we don't know"?

Upon seeing the blind man, Jesus didn't become embroiled in a thorny theological discussion about the human cause of suffering. He prepared to heal the blind man. But first he provided an explanatory comment: "As long as it is day, we must do the work of him who sent me. Night is coming, when no one can work" (John 9:4).

Jesus knew he had only six months left to complete his Father's work. The time to act was now.

Jesus knew he had only six months left to complete his Father's work. The time to act was now.

The Lord felt a divine compulsion to seize the moment for his Father. And he included his disciples in the call to action when he said, "*We* must do the work of him who sent me." As we saw in the last chapter, both their mission and ours is an outgrowth of the ministry given to Jesus by the Father (John 20:21).

After Jesus opened the blind man's eyes, the Pharisees suggested the entire episode was a hoax—that the man had never been blind. Only after he and his parents testified did the religious leaders relent. But they later threw the healed man out of the synagogue for insisting Jesus was from God and sarcastically asking if they, the Pharisees, wanted to become his followers. The healed man had an edge—a sharp sense of humor the religious leaders didn't appreciate. It seems Jesus had healed a man who knew how to laugh in the worst of situations.

The episode infuriated the Pharisees, who insisted Jesus could not have come from God because he violated the no-work-on-the-Sabbath rule by healing on that day. The miracle was later followed by a confrontation with the Pharisees in which Jesus asserted his divinity (John 10:30). Now the Jews no longer saw Jesus as only a violator of the Sabbath, but also a blasphemer, since he claimed to be God. Enraged, they picked up stones to kill him (John 10:31).

What If Jesus Had Procrastinated?

The conflict with the Pharisees might have been avoided, or at least delayed, if Jesus had waited until Sunday to heal the man. Why get into a fight when he could walk away and return the next day? Wouldn't such a delay have been prudent? After all, the beggar probably would have been working the same area the following day. Surely one more day of blindness wouldn't have mattered. And yet, Jesus felt compelled to heal the man on *that* day, a Sabbath, knowing the trouble it would cause.

False excuses and the path of least resistance

One characteristic of procrastinators is they tend to take the path of least resistance. In Proverbs 22:13, Solomon speaks of a man who refuses to start or finish a job because he fears a lion in the street will kill him. My guess is that someone saw the man's farm overgrown with weeds and asked why he hadn't prepared it for crops.

"I'm not crazy," he may have said. "There's a lion running wild, and I could be killed. I'd rather be alive and hungry than dead and full."

And what about the sluggard's neighbors? They faced the same danger yet worked their fields and planted crops. They knew they had to work if they wanted to survive. If necessary, they would have hunted down the lion and killed it. They wouldn't have allowed a false excuse to keep them from completing their work.

Here is the key distinction between procrastinators and people of action: Procrastinators are looking for an excuse to postpone undesirable tasks.

Here is the key distinction between procrastinators and people of action: Procrastinators are *looking* for an excuse to postpone undesirable tasks. Unfortunately, they become so skilled at justifying their behavior that they actually believe the excuses they create. Or maybe believing their own lies is why they're so skilled at inventing them.

Dishonesty and a wrong focus

Solomon approaches the comparison from a different angle when he writes, "The way of the sluggard is blocked with thorns, but the path of the upright is a highway" (Proverbs 15:19). Both men are looking down the same path, yet they see different things. The sluggard sees his pathway filled with thorny obstacles, while the upright man sees an open highway. The problem isn't that the sluggard's path is filled with thorns, but that he imagines it is. Even an open highway may have a few bumps, but the bumps are all the sluggard sees. He doesn't see the highway, he sees the potential obstacles and uses these small problems to justify inaction, laziness, and procrastination.

When we procrastinate, we lie to ourselves to avoid work instead of facing the facts.

Procrastinators focus on problems; the diligent focus on solutions. There is an element of dishonesty in procrastination. When we procrastinate, we lie to ourselves to avoid work instead of facing the facts. We lack the integrity to admit we would rather delay action then expend energy. We aren't mature enough to recognize that the cause of all of our never-started/never-finished projects isn't our circumstances. It's our character.

When we procrastinate, we treat all time alike. We act as if we don't know that each season requires different work. To have food for winter, crops must first be planted, cultivated, harvested, and stored. If we defer any of those steps, we'll come up empty, like the

Egyptian king about whom God said, "He has missed his opportunity" (Jeremiah 46:17).

Jesus knew that every moment was unique. When the Father presented an opportunity to carry out his will, he knew he had to act. He couldn't let opposition drive him to delay what had to be done right away.

The great English playwright and poet William Shakespeare wrote of strategic moments that must be grabbed at once:

> *There is a tide in the affairs of men,*
> *Which, taken at the flood, leads on to fortune;*
> *Omitted, all the voyage of their life*
> *Is bound in shallows and in miseries.*
> *On such a full sea are we now afloat;*
> *And we must take the current when it serves,*
> *Or lose our ventures.*[14]

When the tide is high, it's time to board the ship and begin the voyage. The tide won't wait—and neither will strategic opportunities to be used by God. When we see opportunities to carry out the Father's work, we must act.

The Jesus Experiment

What did Jesus feel and think?

Though the Bible doesn't say what Jesus felt prior to healing the man born blind, other accounts of similar healings do. For instance, when two blind men beside a road asked Jesus to open their eyes, the text says, "Jesus had compassion on them and touched their eyes. Immediately they received their sight and followed him" (Matthew 20:34). Compassion was always the primary emotion that drove

Jesus to relieve the suffering of those he encountered. And it should be our primary emotion as well.

Because Jesus felt a strong urgency, he said, "We *must* do the work of him who sent me" (John 9:4, emphasis added). The act of healing wasn't optional. Jesus felt that he and his disciples had to carry out the Father's work *today*, not tomorrow. This sense of urgency compelled him to act immediately.

Compassion was always the primary emotion that drove Jesus to relieve the suffering of those he encountered. And it should be our primary emotion as well.

Jesus walked in moment-by-moment obedience and communion with his Father. God in turn directed his Son's path, step by step, providing opportunities to demonstrate God's power. By bringing light from darkness in the healing of the man born blind, Jesus illustrated that what we see as infirmities are areas where God can act.

What I feel and think

Most of my procrastination involves little chores that turn into big ones when put off long enough. Faced with such tasks, I feel a sense of dread. This dread is fueled by faulty thinking that either tells me not to worry because it's not a pressing problem or whispers in my ear that magic word: *mañana*.

A few years ago, I noticed that a wooden walkway on our deck was uneven. I knew it would take time—at least five minutes—to check the support post. I'd have to climb down a steep incline to get under the deck, then back up the hill to examine the problem. That didn't sound like fun, so I didn't do it. Every time I walked over the cedar planks, I noticed the slant, but I put off fixing it. I wasn't busy, just lazy.

A couple of months later, while walking across the same spot on the deck, I experienced a moment of inspiration. Knowing such opportunities are rare, I expended the energy and climbed under the deck. That's when I made a . . . well, smelly discovery. Seems the support post had been sunk over the main sewer line exiting the house. Over time, it had crushed the plastic PVC pipe, causing the post to sink a few inches. I wish I could say that was the worst of the problems. It wasn't. Instead of being able to simply jack up the walkway and replace the sinking post with a longer one, I now had a sewage problem, one that had gotten worse over the previous two months as a tiny flow of raw waste, hidden by vegetation, crept across my yard and into the ravine below.

Did I mention the foul bouquet that greeted me when I began repairing the pipe and post?

Solomon described me and my mess when he wrote Proverbs 6:9-11:

> How long will you lie there, you sluggard?
> When will you get up from your sleep?
> A little sleep, a little slumber,
> a little folding of the hands to rest—
> and poverty will come on you like a bandit
> and scarcity like an armed man.

Of course, poverty didn't creep up on me like a bandit; sewage did. Still, my thoughts mimicked the sluggard's. I figured I could put off fixing the problem a little while longer. I had no intention of delaying an inspection for years—only days, weeks, months.

Seek to view every task and human encounter as a divine appointment.

As you live the Jesus Experiment, try to identify the feelings behind procrastination while correcting your faulty thinking. Seek to view every task and human encounter as a divine appointment. I use the word *seek* because it isn't something most of us are conditioned to do. But we can learn how to determine which encounters must be acted on immediately and which can wait. As we abide in Christ, we must remember that God has directed our circumstances so he can use our actions to accomplish our mission to seek and save the lost.

What did Jesus say and do?

Jesus' words tell us he saw the encounter with the blind man as more than just another healing. It was an opportunity to bring light to a man living in literal darkness. In the process, he demonstrated what he offers to those living in spiritual darkness. That's why he said, "As long as it is day, we must do the work of him who sent me. Night is coming, when no one can work. While I am in the world, I am the light of the world" (John 9:4-5).

He followed this statement by healing the man. As we've seen throughout this chapter, Jesus didn't procrastinate when it came to doing his Father's will. He took immediate action.

What I say and do

Most of us have heard numerous lectures on time management, and we all probably understand the importance of creating a daily to-do list, prioritizing it, and then completing the hardest tasks first while avoiding distractions. These are helpful concepts, but we also need to face the truth that following Jesus isn't about a to-do list or setting priorities. It's about asking God to give us the wisdom to view life as he did.

> "Show me, O LORD, my life's end and the number of my days; let me know how fleeting is my life."

Though Jesus knew he had to live with a sense of urgency because his time was limited, he kept his focus on God—doing only what he saw his Father doing and speaking only what he heard his Father saying (John 5:19; 14:10). He expected daily opportunities to minister to people and situations needing immediate action. And he seized every opportunity the Father brought his way.

During this stage of the Jesus Experiment, remind yourself often of David's words in Psalm 39:4: "Show me, O LORD, my life's end and the number of my days; let me know how fleeting is my life." I memorized this verse years ago and review it regularly. Don't get me wrong; I don't think we should live with an internal countdown clock. But I do think we are wise to recognize that life is limited, and as each day closes, our life is one day shorter and death one day nearer. As it says in Ephesians 5:15-16: "Be very careful, then, how you live—not as unwise but as wise, making the most of every opportunity."

The second thing we must do is ask God to give us the wisdom to know which opportunities we must seize and which we must let pass.

Several weeks ago, my hot tub heater quit working. I called the repairman, and he sent out Boris, a man sporting a bushy red beard. He spent a half hour on the spa and fixed the heater and broken ozonator. He hadn't been gone long before I noticed the ozonator, which helps purify the water, had stopped working again.

A few days later, Boris returned to fix it. Curious about his beard, I asked how long he'd had it. He said six months. Then he told me he was Russian Orthodox and was growing it so he could join the church and be baptized.

"Think you'll make it to heaven?" I asked.

"Sure hope so. If I'm good enough."

I paused a moment as I heard a voice of doubt in my mind, telling me to wait until Boris was more comfortable around me before I shared the gospel. But I pushed it away, recognizing God had provided this opportunity and I had to act. *Now.*

"Boris, I've got some great news for you," I said with a smile.

He stopped what he was doing and looked at me. "What's that?"
"You don't have to be good enough."

Over the next twenty minutes, I explained how Christ paid for our sins through his death and three days later rose from the dead. While Boris already knew that, he didn't understand that Christ's payment for his sins was complete and there were no good deeds he had to do to win God's acceptance (Romans 6:23; 2 Corinthians 5:14-15). I told him he could be sure he was going to heaven if he would accept Christ's payment for his sins (Ephesians 2:8-9). Sensing a little confusion, I clarified the difference between intellectual assent and faith as the contrast between a man thinking a plane will fly and actually boarding the plane. At the end of our conversation, Boris climbed aboard.

I paused a moment as I heard a voice of doubt in my mind; but I pushed it away, recognizing God had provided this opportunity and I had to act. **Now.**

Writing this chapter alerted me to the reality that God was working in Boris's life, preparing his heart. As he talked about trying to win God's approval, I felt compassion. And I knew I needed to seize the opportunity, because I might not see him again, or maybe next time I saw him the topic wouldn't come up.

The next week, Cindy was at a Bible study when she met a Russian Orthodox woman who had recently come to Christ along with her husband. Cindy and I knew what we had to do—invite both couples over for dinner.

Living the Jesus Experiment, we must take action when opportunities arise. Someone wisely said, "On the Plains of Hesitation bleach the bones of countless millions, who, at the Dawn of Victory, sat down to wait, and waiting—died."[15]

Better still, the words of Jesus in John 9:4: "As long as it is day, we must do the work of him who sent me. Night is coming when no one can work."

Living the Jesus Experiment

This Week

As you encounter a desire to procrastinate, ask yourself, what would Jesus feel, think, say, and do in this situation? Now take note of your own responses. What are you feeling, thinking, saying, and doing? As you abide in Christ, pray that God will enable you to follow the example of Jesus and take action to share your faith when opportunities arise.

Ask

Read John 5:19-24 and John 9:1-41. On the chart on page 149, examine the left-hand column, noting what Jesus felt, thought, said, and did about taking action.

What motivated Jesus to take action, according to John 5:19 and 9:4?

_____

_____

_____

_____

_____

What opposition to taking action did Jesus face?

_____

_____

_____

_____

_____

Observe

Briefly describe a recent, specific situation when you didn't take action because you were self-focused.

_____

_____

_____

_____

_____

Fill in the center column of the chart (p. 149), recording how you felt, thought, spoke, and acted in that situation when you were self-focused.

Evaluate

In John 15:4-5, how does Jesus tell us we can align with him and learn to take fruitful action?

_____

_____

_____

_____

_____

What stimulates procrastination and holds you back from seizing opportunities? Check those that apply and add your own.

___ Resistance

___ False excuses

___ Dishonesty with myself and others

___ Man-made rules

___ Misunderstanding the opportunity

___ Unimportant details of life

__ Other opportunities
__ Other (be specific) _____

Fill in the right-hand column of the chart, recording what you would feel, think, say, and do in that same situation if you took action while abiding in Christ.

Apply

What are some actions you sense the Lord would have you take in the next week or so? What will you do to complete them?

_____

_____

_____

_____

Write specific steps you will take to overcome procrastination and prepare yourself for the next time God prompts you to take action. Spend a few minutes in prayer, asking God to guide you.

_____

_____

_____

_____

Here are a few ideas to get you started:

- Memorize a motivational verse to help you overcome procrastination and seize opportunities in Christ. For example, you might choose Psalm 39:4: "Show me, O Lord, my life's end and the number of my days; let me know how fleeting is my life."

- Discuss your tendency to procrastinate with a friend or small group and ask someone to question you next week about how you did at seizing opportunities.
- Make a list of the jobs you don't like and tend to put off. Check them off as you complete them.
- Develop specific strategies for overcoming inaction and abiding in Jesus. Rehearse how you will act in a specific situation.
- Place a reminder of your strategy on a frequently viewed surface, such as a mirror or computer screen.

One Week Later

Record your thoughts about how living the Jesus Experiment helped you abide in Jesus and take action over the last seven days. As you've followed Jesus, how has it made your life more fulfilling?

_____

_____

_____

_____

_____

_____

_____

_____

_____

_____

_____

_____

_____

_____

_____

_____

REGARDING TAKING ACTION		
What did Jesus . . .	**What do I . . .**	
Feel? Compassion toward the man born blind and his parents, who were assumed to have caused his blindness. Joy at the healed man's response, and maybe anger toward the Pharisees for their false accusations and proud spiritual blindness. (John 5:19-24; 9:1-41)	*Feel when self-reliant?*	*Feel when abiding in Jesus?*
Think? Possibly Jesus thought this was a work prepared for him to glorify his Father's name. It was a chance to help the people see that he could bring light into darkness.	*Think when self-reliant?*	*Think when abiding in Jesus?*
Say? "Neither this man nor his parents sinned, but this has happened so that the work of God might be displayed in his life. As long as it is day, we must do the work of him who sent me. Night is coming, when no one can work." (John 9:3-4)	*Say when self-reliant?*	*Say when abiding in Jesus?*
Do? "He spit on the ground, made some mud with the saliva, and put it on the man's eyes." (John 9:6)	*Do when self-reliant?*	*Do when abiding in Jesus?*

Download full-size charts and study questions at www.jesusexperiment.com.

He Unexpectedly Helped Others

THOUGH I LIKE MOST MUSIC, I developed a fondness for country and western while growing up in New Mexico and Texas. Someone once called it "the workin' man's blues." The lyrics often communicate the pain of living with too little money and too many bills:

> *I paid the bank note, the car note, and yes, I paid the phone*
> > *bill too.*
> *And then I turned around and I found that the house note's due.*
> *Well, I'd love to take you out like I said I would, honey,*
> *But there's too much month at the end of the money.*[16]

It's been a few years, but I recall a time when those lyrics described my life. Due to a paycheck that didn't keep up with inflation and unexpected expenses, Cindy and I faced a $600 monthly shortfall. My wife clipped coupons, and we learned to enjoy dog-food casserole. Well, it wasn't that bad, but we did cut our expenses. Still, I saw no way out of the fast-approaching financial sinkhole threatening to swallow our home with us inside.

And then something mysterious happened. I received a check for $600 from a church in Livingston, Texas—a town I'd never even passed through. *Happy* doesn't quite capture how I felt about this unexpected gift. I was *exuberant*—"joyously unstrained and enthusiastic."[17] At the last possible moment, from out of the blue, someone had filled the sinkhole with money.

Naturally, the check spurred my curiosity. Who would give me so much money at exactly my time of greatest need? I hadn't discussed our financial situation with anyone except God. The anonymous donor couldn't have known about our need. That is, unless God had quietly informed him.

A month later, the sinkhole reappeared and was growing fast. I lost sleep worrying about how my kids would feel wearing donated hand-me-downs while their friends wore designer jeans and Air Jordans. The month would have been less stressful if I had known another envelope from Livingston would show up in my mailbox.

Never in my life have I experienced greater evidence of God's providential care than those twelve unexpected gifts.

Once again—and for the next ten months—this unexpected gift averted disaster.

One year after the arrival of the first check, I received a $7,200 annual pay raise—that's right, $600 a month. My first thought was, *Hey, I'll be able to save the $600 from Texas.* But the checks stopped coming. Every day for a couple of weeks, I looked in the mailbox, hoping for another check. But the pipeline had run dry.

You might think I would have been disappointed, and I was for a short time. Then my disappointment turned to wonder. God used an unnamed friend to meet a need until the need no longer existed. Never in my life have I experienced greater evidence of God's providential care than those twelve unexpected gifts.

The only thing that rivals the joy of receiving unexpected help is the joy of spontaneously helping. I began thinking about this chapter while traveling to India to visit a boardinghouse orphanage. I figured I'd have plenty of chances to help someone at one of the homes. And I looked for opportunities. But the staff refused to let me help. I was their guest, and they insisted on caring for me.

I love to cook, but they wouldn't let me in the kitchen. The good things I did—playing with children, giving gifts, and providing computers and software for an English lab—were all expected. I left disappointed that, in such a needy setting, I found no way to help in unexpected ways. Such an idea probably sounds crazy.

On my flight home through New Delhi, I managed to get exit row seats for myself and my three traveling companions. As I stretched out, my bliss was suddenly interrupted by a rough jostling on my seat back. I figured it was probably a child banging to the beat of a song. I also thought it would stop. When it didn't, I peered between my seat and the one to my right. A glance at a child usually solves the problem. But I didn't see a child, I saw a giant. Not good. Wanting to better assess his size, I leaned to my left, over the center aisle, and glanced back at his legs. He was so tall his elephant-size legs were pulled up almost to his chest.

I felt the Spirit of God nudge me. I tried to ignore it, but I couldn't. I started wondering what Jesus would feel in the same situation. What would he think?

As I turned away, I felt the Spirit of God nudge me. I tried to ignore it, but I couldn't. I started wondering what Jesus would feel in the same situation. What would he think?

I squirmed as truth battled with comfort. I had prayed for a chance to help someone spontaneously, yet now I was disappointed that God wanted me to give up my exit row seat—*unexpectedly*. I had hoped helping wouldn't require sacrifice. My mind raced to justify my resistance.

I need this seat, I've got bad knees.

He probably wouldn't accept my offer; he's already settled in his seat.

God should have let me fix breakfast for the staff—or save a child from a lion.

I don't want to give up my seat. Anything but my seat!

I glanced once more at the bearlike man. And then something funny happened. Seeing him squeezed into that tiny space made me feel compassion—and a sudden joy as I agreed to follow God's idea.

When the plane reached altitude and the pilot turned off the seat belt sign, the giant climbed out of his seat to get something from the overhead bin. I quickly hopped out of my seat and into his. With his computer in his hand, he turned back and saw me in his seat. His harsh glance silently told me to move. I stood, and when he looked down at me, like Shaquille O'Neal standing next to Ben Stein in those Comcast commercials, he understood.

"I think it will be better if we switch seats," I said.

He nodded, took my exit row seat, and stretched out his legs.

I later learned he was six feet six and weighed three hundred pounds. But he wasn't overweight, just big. At the baggage claim, I saw him walking with a limp. His knee was worse than mine.

I knew I hadn't done anything quite as dramatic as sending a monthly $600 check, but I had identified my feelings and thoughts and followed the Lord's prompting to unexpectedly help. I had *lived* the Jesus Experiment.

When I got home, I began thinking how often Jesus helped people when they didn't expect it. I concluded that many of his miracles and acts of mercy were unexpected by the recipient and everyone else. For instance:

- Turning water into wine at the wedding of Cana (John 2:1-11)
- Casting demons out of the man from Capernaum (Luke 4:31-37)
- Raising Lazarus from the dead (John 11:1-44)
- Defending the sinful woman who anointed his feet with perfume and tears and washed them with her hair (Luke 7:36-50)

There are enough examples to convince me Jesus regularly surprised people with his generosity. But I found one story especially relevant because the Bible identifies what Jesus felt before he did the unexpected.

A Surprise Picnic

After hearing of the death and burial of his cousin and forerunner, John the Baptist, it's no surprise Jesus wanted to get away with his disciples to a secluded place. With that in mind, they climbed into a boat and set sail toward a deserted area near the town of Bethsaida, on the eastern shore of the Sea of Galilee. They probably would have succeeded in finding solitude if people hadn't spotted their boat and followed from the shoreline, like children chasing a parade (Mark 6:32–33).

When the disciples beached the boat, an excited crowd greeted them. Rather than donning sunglasses and surrounding himself with bodyguards, a weary and grieving Jesus stepped ashore and gazed at the throng of people—possibly numbering as many as fifteen thousand men, women, and children—assembled on the grassy shoreline.

Instead of feeling annoyed that the people had outflanked his escape, Jesus "had compassion on them, because they were like sheep without a shepherd."

155

Instead of feeling annoyed that the people had outflanked his escape, Jesus "had compassion on them, because they were like sheep without a shepherd" (Mark 6:34). I can't help but wonder if Jesus saw John as the nation's spiritual shepherd. With John gone, the people had no one to guide them. Whatever prompted his thoughts, the Lord's compassion compelled him to set aside his grief and fatigue and spend the sunny spring day teaching and healing.

His concern for the people also motivated him to do something unexpected. As evening approached, the disciples urged Jesus to send everyone away so they could find food and lodging (Luke 9:12). This seemed to be good advice, since the day was about gone and they were in a remote place.

Instead, Jesus told the disciples, "They do not need to go away. You give them something to eat" (Matthew 14:16). This would be like having the manager of a fifteen-thousand-seat concert venue ask you and eleven friends to round up a couple of hot dogs and a Coke for all the fans, because the catering company didn't show up. Not an easy job when you're on foot, carry little money, and the closest town is miles away. With luck you might find a boy standing on the edge of the crowd with two hot dogs and a partial package of buns.

When the disciples' search turned up five loaves of bread and two fish, Simon Peter's brother, Andrew, asked the obvious question, "How far will they go among so many?" (John 6:9).

It's at this point that Jesus did the unexpected. After asking the disciples to organize the people into groups of fifty, he took the bread and the fish, gave thanks to God, broke the loaves, and distributed the food to his disciples to feed the crowd. Miraculously, everyone ate and was satisfied, and twelve baskets of bread were left over (Matthew 14:20).

Because we've heard this story so many times, the surprise of the miracle may have worn thin. It's as if we've seen the end of the movie before the beginning. Though we may not be surprised, the crowd was. No one expected Jesus to feed thousands of people—especially with such an empty pantry. The people had followed Jesus to hear his words of wisdom and find healing. Nobody, including the disciples, anticipated dinner.

The Jesus Experiment

What did Jesus feel?

Jesus didn't feed the crowd out of a sense of obligation. Nor was his act a random display of kindness, like buying coffee for the person in line behind you at Starbucks, whether or not that person needs your help. At his emotional core, Jesus felt compassion for the people because they had no one to lead them, teach them, protect them, heal them, or feed them. They had no shepherd. Jesus identified with their suffering and lostness. This emotional connection moved him to put aside his grief and exhaustion so he could care for others.

> *At his emotional core, Jesus felt compassion for the people because they had no one to lead them, teach them, protect them, heal them, or feed them.*

What I feel

What keeps me from unexpectedly helping others is that I often don't think about it. I can be oblivious to other people's pain. I also suffer from compassion fatigue. I'm inundated with images of suffering—hurricane victims, tsunami victims, earthquake victims, flood victims, crime victims, war victims—and emotionally tune out the needs of those around me. This landslide of human hurt is beyond my ability to help—or so it seems. So I disengage: the antithesis of compassion.[18]

To be honest, it's not just the visual images of suffering that close my heart. It's a fear of squandering my resources by investing in a corrupt cause. I've experienced this during visits to India. Walking down a street in Mumbai, I've seen so many suffering people that I've learned to ignore them. Beggars of all ages, with sad brown eyes and outstretched hands, pleading for help. If I make eye contact, they'll follow me for blocks. If I help one, I become a giant star and my gravitational pull attracts other beggars into my orbit, following me like a dozen earths chasing the sun. It's tempting to swat them away, not like humans created in God's image but like gnats.

Jesus may not have helped everyone he encountered, but he felt compassion for everyone, including those who tortured him and nailed him to a cross.

To protect myself from a tsunami of beggars, I become emotionally blind. It leaves me feeling not just inadequate, but guilty. After all, the reason I travel to India is to rescue suffering children.

When I shared my dilemma with a friend, he reminded me that Jesus didn't heal *all* the suffering people in Israel, nor feed *all* the hungry, nor raise *all* the dead. But that truth provides little comfort. I know I can't help everyone; that's not what bothers me. It's my lack of compassion that disturbs me. Jesus may not have helped everyone he encountered, but he felt compassion for *everyone*, including those who tortured him and nailed him to a cross. And it was his compassion that prompted him to help those his Father brought into his life.

I've learned I have to cultivate compassion. One time on the streets of Mumbai, a twentysomething girl approached me, begging for help. She held a baby with filth on his face like war paint. I tried to walk by her, but she stood in my way. Placing the fingers of her right hand against her thumb, she raised her hand to her mouth— the universal sign for "Food. Please."

"No money," I said.

"No money," she said in broken English. "Rice and oil for my baby. Please, rice and oil only."

I was reluctant to give her money because I had no idea what she would do with it; food was another matter. I followed her to a store, where the proprietor pulled a bag of rice and a quart jug of oil from a shelf. I handed him some rupees and waited for my change. Clearly insulted, he threw me an angry look, returned the rupees, and told me to get out. Confused, I went to another store, but the same thing happened.

Outside, on the crowded street, I realized I had been offering Pakistani rupees, which I hadn't converted from a recent trip. Unsure what to do, I gave the beggar an American ten dollar bill—a jackpot for any beggar. Instead of thanking me, she angrily grabbed the money, made an insulting comment, and marched away.

I stood on the edge of the street, bewildered, as I watched her disappear into the crowd like a wisp of smoke.

Bad experiences made me suspicious of the very people I wanted to feel compassion for. Scam artists made it easy to close my heart to the needs of others.

Later, I learned she had scammed me. The beggar and the store worked together. She begged until she found a tourist who would buy her food. Once the tourist was gone, she returned the food, the store owner paid her a commission, and she returned to the streets to hunt for another foreigner to scam. I never figured out why she was upset with the cash. Maybe she knew the store owner would keep it all.

Experiences like that made me suspicious of the very people I wanted to feel compassion for. Scam artists made it easy to close my heart to the needs of others.

Then I had an experience that forever changed my view of beggars—a relational paradigm shift.

During another stay in Mumbai, I hung around some teenage

beggars who lived in a slum and worked the tourist district by the five-star Taj Hotel, the same hotel attacked by terrorists in November 2008.

After a couple of days on the streets with these kids, I felt a connection with them. I talked with a group of boys who peddled kites to make a few rupees a day. I chatted with some girls, dressed in colorful saris, who were amazingly cheerful in the face of hardship. Surprisingly, these kids never asked me for a handout. Then one day, a girl said, "Would you buy some rice and oil for my little brother?"

I smiled and said, "Hey, you're trying to scam me."

"You're right," she said enthusiastically, happy her new American friend had learned a lesson from the street.

Life has taught me that compassion is cultivated in the soil of understanding.

I felt as if we had become friends. I knew her well enough to feel compassion. And that emotion prompted me to do what I had refused to do before—help unexpectedly.

When I saw her horrid living conditions and how hard she and her friends worked for a few rupees, I felt their despair. So I slipped them some money, hoping they would use it to help relieve their suffering. Life has taught me that compassion is cultivated in the soil of understanding.

What did Jesus think, say, and do?

Jesus used situations not only to meet physical needs, but also to teach important lessons. That's why, in the story of the feeding of five thousand men, nothing hooked my attention more than what Jesus said after his disciples urged him to send everyone home. The men had expressed an obvious concern for others, but Jesus wanted to move beyond disengaged compassion to constructive action. That's why he said, "You give them something to eat" (Matthew 14:16).

He might as well have told them to fly. They saw the need but thought they lacked the resources to meet it. But Jesus knew their future ministries would focus on meeting people's needs—spiritual and physical. That's why, after his resurrection, he told Peter, "Feed my sheep" (John 21:17).

When the disciples mentioned they had found five loaves and two fish, Jesus seized this real-life teaching opportunity. "Bring them here to me," he said (Matthew 14:18).

He took the fish and bread, gave thanks to God, and handed the food to the disciples, who gave it to the people. The men may not have realized it then, but later they understood: Before you can give to others, you must first receive from Jesus.

Before you can give to others, you must first receive from Jesus.

The miracle of feeding thousands with a meal intended for one proved that Jesus was the Son of God and the Lord of creation, but it also showed the disciples that Jesus would take what little they had and use it—and them—to unexpectedly meet the needs of others.

What I think, say, and do

Sometimes I see a need I can, but don't want to, meet. If Jesus is going to use me as a conduit of his kindness, I must train myself to think differently. I need to think about how others feel and ask God to show me not only their needs, but how those needs affect them.

With the big man on the airplane, my initial response to the jostling of my seat back was annoyance. I didn't look back hoping to see someone to whom I could extend compassion. I looked back in frustration, hoping a stern stare would stop the aggravation.

But when I saw the man cramped like a wound-up jack-in-the-box, I hurt for him. When I understood the jostling, I understood the jostler. And understanding gave birth to compassion, as it had with the kids in Mumbai. Once I understood the man's situation from his perspective, God's Spirit prompted me to do something unexpected to relieve his discomfort.

Cultivating compassion requires us to abide in Jesus and to remember that most people are like us. Chances are, they're trying to accomplish one of five goals:

- Find happiness: Most people aren't trying to make other people unhappy; they just want to be happy themselves.
- Avoid suffering: People usually don't intend to cause suffering; they merely want to avoid it. The man sitting behind me wasn't trying to jostle my seat; he was trying to fit his legs into the available space.
- Avoid pain, disappointment, loss, loneliness, or despair: If we knew the *why* behind what other people say and do, we might feel sympathy rather than anger.
- Bring a dream into reality: Many people are chasing a dream, and they relate best to people who share their vision. At times, they may become insensitive to those who impede their progress.
- Be understood and accepted: Everyone wants to be known and loved for who they are.

Looking through other people's eyes may grant understanding, leading to compassion. But we still may not think we can meet their needs. That's when we must surrender our resources to the Lord, so he can multiply them to serve others. Unfortunately, though I like to think I've given God my time, talents, and resources, when he nudges me to use them to help someone else I often hesitate. Jesus said, "If you cling to your life, you will lose it; but if you give up your life for me, you will find it" (Matthew 10:39, NLT). In a sense,

Jesus reversed the playground rhyme, "Finders keepers, losers weepers," so it says, "Finders weepers, losers keepers."

We find true joy and happiness when we lose what we own to help someone else. And we do this best when we give all we have to the Lord so he can work through us.

In a sense, Jesus reversed the playground rhyme, "Finders keepers, losers weepers," so it says, "Finders weepers, losers keepers."

In the moment, our focus may be on what we're sacrificing—like an exit row seat. We may think the loss will rob us of comfort and joy. And it might. But research indicates that performing an act of kindness makes the performer happier.[19] And it doesn't matter whether it's a small or big act. You'll be just as happy if you open the door for someone at the grocery store, put a quarter in someone's expired parking meter, compliment a coworker for a job well done, or pay off a student's college loan. If you perform five acts of kindness in one day, it will make you happier than if you do those same acts over five days.[20]

Ultimately, our purpose for treating others kindly isn't because it will make us happy. That's a side benefit. We do it because it's a crucial way Jesus can work though us to touch the lives of those we encounter.

Living the Jesus Experiment

This Week

When you have an opportunity to help someone unexpectedly, ask yourself what Jesus would feel, think, say, and do in the same situation. Now take note of your own responses. What are you feeling, thinking, saying, and doing? As you abide in Jesus this week, pray for an unexpected opportunity to help someone.

Ask

Read Matthew 14:6-21 and Mark 6:30-44. On the chart on page 167, examine the left-hand column, noting what Jesus felt, thought, said, and did about helping people unexpectedly. Matthew 14:14 tells us that as soon as Jesus stepped off the boat, he felt compassion for the crowd, despite having just heard about the death of his cousin, John the Baptist, and despite his desire to seek solace. How do you think Jesus emotionally and mentally moved past his personal loss to attend to the needs of the crowd? How did he unexpectedly help the people and his own disciples? Record your thoughts below.

_____

_____

_____

_____

_____

_____

Observe

On a five-point scale (1 = annoyed, 5 = compassionate) rank how you feel in the following situations.

____ A family member asks for help.

____ A task you delegated at home doesn't get done.

____ A neighbor asks for assistance on a project while you're busy.

____ A coworker asks for a ride home and it's out of your way.

____ In line at Starbucks, the person in front of you places a long order and then realizes he left his wallet at home.

Think of a recent situation in which you were interrupted by someone with a need you could meet. Fill in the center column of the chart (p. 167), recording how you felt, thought, spoke, and acted in response to that need when your focus was on yourself.

Evaluate

Fill in the right-hand column of the chart, recording what you would feel, think, say, and do in that same situation if you were abiding in Jesus and responded as he would.

Apply

Which of the following steps would help prepare you to feel, think, speak, and act like Jesus when you see someone in need?

_____ Memorize verses that help me see the value of caring for and helping others (for example, Mark 6:34; Philippians 2:3-4).

_____ Journal each day for one week how I unexpectedly helped, or didn't help, people with needs I could meet.

_____ Pray for opportunities to unexpectedly help someone.

_____ Ask God to give me compassion for those in need.

_____ Actively look for someone I can unexpectedly help.

Identify some specific ways you could unexpectedly help someone in the next week:

_____

_____

_____

_____

_____

One Week Later

Record your thoughts about how living the Jesus Experiment enabled you to help someone unexpectedly during the past seven days. How has abiding in Jesus and expressing his love in this way made your life more fulfilling?

_____

_____

_____

_____

_____

_____

_____

_____

_____

_____

_____

_____

_____

_____

_____

_____

_____

_____

_____

_____

_____

_____

_____

_____

_____

_____

_____

_____

REGARDING HELPING OTHERS

What did Jesus . . .	What do I . . .	
Feel? He felt compassion when he saw the people without a shepherd. (Mark 6:30-39)	*Feel when self-reliant?*	*Feel when abiding in Jesus?*
Think? Though the text doesn't say, it would seem Jesus thought this was a good teaching moment for the disciples. (Matthew 14:16)	*Think when self-reliant?*	*Think when abiding in Jesus?*
Say? "They do not need to go away. You give them something to eat." (Matthew 14:16) "Bring them here to me." (Matthew 14:18))	*Say when self-reliant?*	*Say when abiding in Jesus?*
Do? Jesus taught, healed, and prepared the disciples for future ministry by showing them he would take what they had and use it, and he fed the crowd. (Matthew 14:13-21)	*Do when self-reliant?*	*Do when abiding in Jesus?*

Download full-size charts and study questions at www.jesusexperiment.com.

What Jesus Did with People

He Served Status Seekers

MY FIRST BEST FRIEND was a boy named John. He lived on Oak Street, one block south of my home on Juniper Street in Roswell, New Mexico. I remember John as a dark-haired kid with blue eyes and freckles. We hung out together and played on the Little League team my dad coached.

My family lived in a house my dad built. I remember it as one of the nicest in town. When I saw it a few years ago, the Austin Stone siding had been stripped from its facade, the huge front window had been replaced by several small ones, the shrubbery that once framed the house was gone, and the sturdy white fence that had enclosed a large, grassy backyard and two graceful willows had been replaced with a shabby wooden one that concealed a collection of junk.

I haven't seen John since I moved from Roswell to Austin when I was sixteen. I hope he's weathered the years better than my childhood home.

One day, when we were seven or eight, John and I started a fire in the alley behind my house. In all the excitement, John got too close to the flames and his shirt caught fire. He panicked and took off running. It was the first time I had seen someone panic, and it scared me.

I had recently learned that when people catch on fire, they should "stop, drop, and roll." So, after John darted off, I chased him down and tackled him, throwing myself on the fire and smothering it. John told me I had saved his life. I don't know if I did . . . probably not. But it felt good for someone to think so.

Even though John and I spent years together, I never *knew* him. We were just kids. What do you actually know about your best childhood friend? I remember something odd that happened after the last day of sixth grade. As soon as the bell rang, John sprinted across the schoolyard and ran home. I followed him to his house, but he rushed inside and slammed the door.

I've heard emotions never grow up. If we remember a childhood experience, we feel it the way we did as children, though we're now adults.

When John didn't invite me in, I didn't feel rejection; I felt fear—as if a snake had bitten him. As I think about that day, I feel the same emotions I felt then. I've heard emotions never grow up. If we remember a childhood experience, we feel it the way we did as children, though we're now adults.

John later told me he had to repeat sixth grade. He was embarrassed to tell me because he feared I would think less of him.

Who Is the Greatest?

John's response that day reflects the status-conscious culture in which we live: We hide our weaknesses, always displaying our shiny sides. We might pretend we're not caught up in all the moving and shaking, but then we say things like, "Second place is first loser" and "Go big or go home." Even our "reality" shows are about competition.

The tendency to measure up and compete—establishing the pecking order—is common among both men and women; they just do it differently. The truth is, we all strive for status and respect in one way or another. At some level, we're all asking, "Did you notice me?" "Would you choose me?" "Do you think I'm good enough, valuable enough, beautiful enough?"

Based on the Jesus Experiment thus far, you might think growing closer to Jesus would make it easier not to contend for status and position—if we truly grasped the meaning of the Cross, maybe it would—but that wasn't the case for the disciples. Right up to the night before Jesus died, they were jockeying for position and seeking to elevate themselves in the coming kingdom.

Three vignettes establish this point.

Mark 9:2-13 records the story of the Transfiguration, which we'll look at more closely in chapter 12. While Jesus, Peter, James, and John were on the mountain, the rest of the disciples were in a nearby village, unsuccessfully trying to heal a demon-possessed boy. After Jesus returned and cast out the demon, he and the disciples continued their journey to Capernaum. Along the way, Jesus spoke about his impending death and resurrection (Mark 9:30-32), but the disciples were caught up in an argument about who was greatest. The proximity of the two stories makes me wonder if perhaps they had been *competing* to see who could cast out the demon from the boy.

Jesus spoke about his impending death and resurrection, but the disciples were caught up in an argument about who was greatest.

In Mark 10:35-45, we read an account of the time James and John approached Jesus and asked for the privilege of sitting at his right and left hand in the coming kingdom. When the other disciples heard about this, "they became indignant" (Mark 10:41). I suspect they wondered, *Why didn't I think of that?*

On the night of the Last Supper, after three years of walking daily with Jesus and soaking in his wisdom and marveling at the miracles he performed, the disciples remained concerned about power and status. As they climbed the stairs to the upper room, I'm sure they were thinking, *Someone is going to get the seat of honor, and someone is going to end up at the other end of the table.*

The Last Supper

When the disciples arrived at the Jerusalem home, they smelled the aroma of roasted lamb and freshly baked bread and saw the room prepared for their arrival—a U-shaped table on the wooden floor, rugs and pillows on which to recline, and a wash basin, a pitcher of water, and a folded towel. The water and towel were to be used by the lowest servant in the house to wash the feet of each guest. But that night, no servant appeared and no disciple volunteered for the job.

Each man quickly looked to the place of honor. Everyone wanted to sit opposite that seat—the number two position.

Instead, each man quickly looked to the place of honor. Everyone wanted to sit opposite that seat—the number two position. They likely migrated to that corner, each coveting it like kids eying a single ice cream cone. It's not hard to imagine Peter staking out the spot, only to be pulled back, like a man who has stepped in front of a bus, by James and John.

An argument erupted as to who among them was greatest.[†] The events of the previous week had created a crescendo of expectations.

[†] Luke 22:23–27 places the argument after they had eaten the Passover—which would make it even more astounding. Whether the argument took place before or after the meal, the disciples entered the room with a competitive spirit, which Jesus addressed.

The disciples believed Jesus would soon usher in his kingdom and they were destined for greatness in his administration. The question remained: Who would be his chief of staff?

As each man debated the merits of his case, comparing credentials and résumés, the door opened and Jesus entered. Immediately, the argument ended.

Picturing the scene in the upper room reminds me of an experience I had in fourth grade. Parkview Elementary School had a single hall that ran from one end of the building to the other. Whenever our teacher, Mrs. Harris, left the classroom, we set a guard at the door to peek through the crack and keep watch for her return. In her absence, we had wadded-up paper fights and spitball wars. We danced. We partied. We had a blast during those blessed moments of freedom. But as soon as our lookout spotted Mrs. Harris slowly returning down the long hallway, we scooped up the mess and sat in our chairs like a class of angels. She entered a room of closed-casket silence and laser-like focus.

Jesus reminded his disciples that, in his kingdom, the greatest would be least and the meek most powerful.

Unlike Mrs. Harris, Jesus knew exactly what was going on with his disciples. But he didn't scold or punish them, as Mrs. Harris would have done had she arrived in the middle of one of our parties. Instead, he reminded his disciples that, in his kingdom, the greatest would be least and the meek most powerful.

On the TV show *Undercover Boss*, the CEO of Frontier Airlines concealed his identity and took a job cleaning planes, including dumping sewage and cleaning up vomit. He did this to see firsthand the true condition of his company and its employees. This is a powerful illustration of the leader becoming the least. In the kingdom of God, serving others isn't a temporary undercover role, it's a way of life that sees beauty in service, power in humility.

The disciples quietly reclined, probably waiting for Jesus to pray or lead in the singing of a psalm. But he didn't. In fact, he did the last thing they expected—as surprising as exploding a firecracker.

Jesus removed his outer garments, girded himself with a towel, poured water into the basin, and knelt before his disciples. Then he washed their dirty, grimy, and smelly feet.

The disciples anticipated this about as much as they expected a tuxedo-clad bear to walk through the door, tap dance for a few minutes, and serve them steaming lobster. It would be like the queen of England shining her guests' shoes at a state dinner.

I've studied and taught this story countless times. I've expounded on the servant spirit of Jesus and encouraged others to follow his lead. But it wasn't until the other night that I recognized possibly the most important aspect of this story. You see, I had a dream that showed me something I'd never seen before. It wasn't a plasma-screen HD dream. It was shadowy, the kind of dream where, no matter how hard you try to focus, you can't. Everything was blurry and slow.

Service isn't just a kind act. Service is an indescribably beautiful picture of Jesus.

In this dream, I saw one person washing another person's feet. Even though the images were out of focus, I realized I was in the presence of something indescribably beautiful. I don't mean admirable or commendable; I mean transcendently magnificent. The man washing the feet seemed to be strong and distinguished. Yet at the same time, the one being served looked shrunken. Not unsightly, but undesirable by comparison.

It was a deeply spiritual dream. Because I had been studying this story, I believe God showed me something I otherwise wouldn't have seen. When I awoke, I knew I had experienced an epiphany that shifted my perspective: *Service isn't just a kind act. Service is an indescribably beautiful picture of Jesus.*

In the following days, whenever I observed an act of service, even something as small as opening a door for someone or picking up a piece of trash and placing it in a trash bin, I thought, *That was a beautiful act.* The dream had a profound effect on me.

The Jesus Experiment

What did Jesus feel and think?

Jesus entered the upper room knowing his closest friends would abandon him and he would suffer the most horrifying death in human history. Judas would betray him, Peter would deny him, the disciples would desert him, and the Jews would arrest him, try him, and hand him over to the Romans, who would crucify him. Talk about emotional and psychological weight. In spite of the betrayal by his closest friends, we're told that when "Jesus knew that his hour had come to depart out of this world to the Father, having loved his own who were in the world, he loved them to the end" (John 13:1, ESV).

Jesus entered the upper room loving his disciples and picturing how he could both demonstrate his love and provide an unforgettable example of what greatness is in his kingdom. Never again would a servant wash the disciples' feet without it reminding them of the Lord's example of servant leadership. Never again would they imagine achieving greatness without knowing they must serve like their Savior. And never again would they forget Jesus' love.

> *Never again would a servant wash the disciples' feet without it reminding them of the Lord's example of servant leadership.*

What I feel and think

Sometimes, showing respect demands an act of service that goes above and beyond the call of duty. My friend Robert E. Farrell launched more than 150 successful restaurants in the Pacific

Northwest and across the United States. Bob was a pioneer in exceeding a customer's expectations long before it became a business catchphrase. "Give 'em the pickle . . . and they'll be back" was not only the title of his book, but also his way of saying that if you do what it takes to make your customers happy, they'll remain loyal to your business.

Years ago, Bob's commitment to customer service was put to the test when an unhappy customer came to the cash register at a Farrell's ice cream parlor. The man had brought his six-year-old son in for a free ice cream sundae, but through a miscommunication between the hostess and the server, the boy's sundae never arrived.

Bob was manning the cash register, and when the father handed him the bill, Bob could tell he was upset. The father insisted everything was fine, and wanted to pay his tab. When Bob told him he owned the restaurant and would do everything possible to make things right, the man shouted at him, "You can't straighten it out! It's too late!"

When someone disrespects me by raising his or her voice, it usually makes me defensive. I feel like pushing back and demanding the person calm down. Not Bob. Instead, he pleaded with the man to let him fix the problem.

Finally, the father told Bob why he was angry. Even more than the sundae, his son had been looking forward to everyone singing for him.

"Sir, I'm very sorry," Bob said. "And I'm going to make it up to you right now."

Without a moment's hesitation, he lifted the boy onto the counter, grabbed a sundae, and handed it to the boy.

"What's your name?" he asked.

"Alex."

"How old are you, Alex?"

"I'm six years old," he said with a big smile.

Bob called for the attention of everyone in the restaurant and said, "We're all going to sing 'Happy Birthday' to Alex, who is six years old today."

With that, he led the assembled customers and employees in a rousing rendition of the birthday song. What began as a potential disaster ended as a birthday Alex would never forget.[21]

Why did Bob respond that way? Because he firmly believed that every customer should be treated with the status of a celebrity . . . *even a six-year-old boy.* Bob's job as the owner wasn't to be served by his employees and customers. His job was to serve them.

He firmly believed that every customer should be treated with the status of a celebrity . . . even a six-year-old boy.

It's one thing to hear an inspiring story and another thing to embrace a philosophy of conferring status by serving.

What did Jesus say and do?

When Jesus walked in on his disciples' argument about who was the greatest, at first he didn't say a word. He didn't have to; his actions spoke volumes: "You want to see greatness? You want to see power? Look here. I've been telling you all along that those who would be great must serve. Well, this is what it looks like."

Does it fascinate you, as it does me, that on the last evening of Jesus' earthly life, at a time when he surely felt the urgency of the hour, he didn't review his accomplishments? He didn't remind his disciples about the people he had healed, fed, taught, forgiven, or raised from the dead. He didn't talk about walking on water or driving out demons. He didn't perform one last miracle. Instead, he disrobed, knelt, and did the work of a slave.

You may know the story: When Jesus got to Peter, the fisherman said, "No . . . you shall never wash my feet" (John 13:8).

I have to admit, I don't blame Peter. Jesus was the Messiah, the future king. From Peter's perspective, kings didn't wash the feet of fishermen. They ruled kingdoms. They commanded armies.

In creating the role of servant leader, Jesus modeled what the apostle Paul later called "power . . . made perfect in weakness."

Peter may have thought Jesus had lost his mind. No leader had ever performed such a humiliating task. What Peter didn't realize was that Jesus was redefining leadership, power, and greatness. In creating the role of servant leader, Jesus modeled what the apostle Paul later called "power . . . made perfect in weakness" (2 Corinthians 12:9).

Whatever Peter thought, his words were a veiled rebuke—a pushback against Jesus. In response, the Lord pushed back harder. He said, "Unless I wash you, you have no part with me" (John 13:8). In other words, "I either wash your feet or show you the door."

Given that choice, Peter relented.

In his initial refusal, Peter had apparently forgotten what happened when James and John asked Jesus if they could sit at his right and left during his future glory. The Lord had called the disciples together and told them,

> You know that those who are regarded as rulers of the Gentiles lord it over them, and their high officials exercise authority over them. Not so with you. Instead, whoever wants to become great among you must be your servant, and whoever wants to be first must be slave of all. For even the Son of Man did not come to be served, but to serve, and to give his life as a ransom for many.
>
> MARK 10:42-45

With the washing of the disciples' feet, Jesus had *demonstrated* what he meant. And then he said, "I have set you an example that you should do as I have done for you. I tell you the truth, no servant is greater than his master, nor is a messenger greater than the one who sent him. Now that you know these things, you will be blessed if you do them" (John 13:15-17).

Unfortunately, many people in our culture, even in the church, view servanthood as a sign of passivity or weakness. And yet, from Jesus' perspective, it's a badge of strength. It often requires more internal strength, more strength of character, to serve than to be served.

Jesus always interacted with people from a position of strength and self-control. Yet he exercised that strength not by dominating, but by serving. In John's account of the footwashing, he gives us insight into the source of Jesus' strength: "Jesus knew that the Father had put all things under his power, and that he had come from God and was returning to God" (John 13:3). His humility and sense of worth flowed from his Father, who completely and absolutely affirmed him. That freed Jesus to serve others without regard to appearances.

Jesus always interacted with people from a position of strength and self-control. Yet he exercised that strength not by dominating, but by serving.

How did Jesus lead? He didn't seek honor—he extended it. He didn't crave respect—he gave it. The disciples, like we do, tried in their own strength to lead by fighting for honor and refusing to serve. They hadn't yet learned how to find their identity in Christ. Jesus didn't fight for a position of honor because his Father had already showered him with honor. Now he honored his disciples.

By washing the disciples' feet, Jesus did more than remove the day's dirt. He lifted the disciples above himself—even Judas, the betrayer. If the Messiah would stoop to serve them, it speaks volumes about their worth. I imagine, after Jesus' resurrection and ascension, the disciples often reflected on this amazing demonstration of respect. Without a doubt, knowing that Jesus loved and respected them fueled their ability and desire to dedicate their lives to carrying out their mission.[22]

What I say and do

It's easy to look at the disciples with all their infighting and grandstanding and think, *Boy, they really didn't get it, did they?* But their arguments don't surprise me. I identify with them. Don't you?

> *It's easy to look at the disciples with all their infighting and grandstanding and think,* Boy, they really didn't get it, did they?

I attended a meeting of Christian leaders at the White House several years ago. I wanted a seat in front, so I slipped by some of the most prominent Christian leaders in the country to get a better seat. Of course, I performed my act of self-advancement with the slick nonchalance of a subway pickpocket. Nobody noticed—except my friend Bob, who watched as I unabashedly ignored the rules of common courtesy. Then he followed me. We weren't going to wait for seats of honor; we would take one. Just like the disciples.

Later that evening, my son Paul, who worked as a junior staffer at the White House, took me on a private tour of the West Wing. When he showed me the Oval Office, I stood in the doorway, staring in awe. I tried to imagine what it would be like to be the most powerful man on earth. As I gazed in wonder, Paul spotted another staffer and stepped aside to talk to him. As the two engaged in a lively conversation, they walked into the Roosevelt Room, across the hall from the Oval Office.

I looked to my left and right, up and down the hall. I was alone. Not a single Secret Service agent in sight. And then I did the craziest thing I've ever done. I stepped across the threshold and walked briskly to the famous Resolute desk, the one nearly every president has used since Rutherford B. Hayes in 1880. I've got to tell you, it was an adrenaline rush. I knew it was risky, but I figured the worst thing they would do was throw me out and lecture my son. And I was sure that was a sacrifice Paul would be willing to make for his father.

I expected several Secret Service agents to rush into the room at any moment and escort me out. When nobody showed up, I walked behind the desk and stood next to the president's black leather-tufted chair. Still . . . no agents. I couldn't believe it. My heart beat like a racing rabbit's—I figure 180 beats a minute—as I contemplated the unthinkable . . . sitting in the president's chair. Time was of the essence. In a nanosecond—which is one billionth of a second—I decided to go for it. I swiveled the president's chair around, sat down, leaned back, and in one swift motion placed my feet on the solid timber surface of the desktop.

I considered lifting the phone off its cradle and calling home but decided that might be pushing it. Instead, I leaned back a little further, closed my eyes, and imagined the world at my feet.

Just then, I became aware of the presence of someone else in the room. I opened my eyes as a uniformed security office grabbed hold of my right foot and violently pulled my leg.

Just like I'm pulling *yours*.

Yes, I cut in line at a White House meeting of Christian leaders. And yes, my son took me on a private evening tour of the West Wing. But no, I did not sneak into the Oval Office and sit at the president's desk—though the thought crossed my mind.

When I tell that story to a live audience, people gasp at the

What kind of person would sneak into the Oval Office and sit behind the president's desk? Probably a person crazy enough to vie for a position at the right hand of the Son of God.

audacity of my act. They sit up with wide-eyed, open-mouthed disbelief. What kind of person would sneak into the Oval Office and sit behind the president's desk? Well, probably a person crazy enough to vie for a position at the right hand of the Son of God. I can assure you, the throne room of God outclasses even the Oval Office. Yet James and John were ready to walk right in there.

How about cutting in line to get a seat near the front row? I'm embarrassed to admit I did that. I think I demonstrated the kind of disrespect the disciples showed when they competed for the seat of honor at the Last Supper. Of course, their rush for the best seat meant they wouldn't have to wash any dirty feet, a job no one wanted except for the guest of honor, the head of the table—Jesus.

The disciples sought respect in a seat of honor. I sought a place of honor by cutting in line. Jesus *demonstrated* both respect and honor in the lowly role of a servant. Did you catch that last point?

While writing this chapter, I've prayed for a situation where I could put this principle into practice. I wasn't sure what that situation would look like. And until it was over, I didn't realize the extent of what had happened.

My friend Vic

About a month ago, I received an e-mail from an old friend, Vic, whom I hadn't seen in more than ten years. He's a bear of a man with a brilliant mind, quick sense of humor, and tender heart. He was undergoing knee replacement surgery and wanted me to know. Even though we hadn't talked in a long time, we have the kind of friendship that allows us to pick up where we left off, as if no time had passed. So I decided to pay him a hospital visit.

Standing next to his bedside, I asked about his son, a cancer survivor. Vic said he was doing well. That's why I was surprised when, three weeks later, just as I returned from a trip to the East

Coast and just as I sat down to work on this chapter, I checked my e-mail and saw one from Vic telling me his son had relapsed and was in the hospital.

I immediately grabbed the phone and called Vic. When he answered, he said he was in the surgical waiting room, nervously wringing his hands. He said things had gone badly; the surgery had lasted eight hours and the physicians hadn't excised the entire tumor. There was so much bleeding that the doctor had to stop the surgery to control it. They would try to finish two days later—*if* his son had sufficiently recovered.

If not, he might die.

I felt compelled to get in my car and drive across town to Legacy Hospital. But I knew Vic was with

Have you noticed how life has a way of intruding on our best-laid plans?

his family, most of whom I didn't know. I feared I'd be intruding, so I asked if I should come. Vic encouraged me to drop by in a day or so, maybe during the next surgery.

Have you noticed how life has a way of derailing our best-laid plans? When the date of the follow-up surgery arrived, my schedule was packed and so was my suitcase. Not only was I preparing to fly away, the hospital was across town in northeast Portland. I wanted to see Vic, but the thought of fighting traffic tempted me just to call for an update and skip the visit. After all, we had seen each other only once or twice in the last decade. But I have a deep and enduring love for my friend and wanted to see him. I wanted to be with him as his son battled for his life.

I found Vic and his family in the hospital waiting room. The procedure had been delayed, so we visited and talked about old times. I prayed for Vic and his son. Everyone was in tears, and I hugged them all before leaving. The following day, Vic's son had the surgery and everything went well. He's now recovering.

I realize my hospital visit was a small gesture—in fact, I hesitated to mention it. But that was the situation that faced me as I lived the Jesus Experiment that week. Had I allowed my selfishness to hold me back, as I so often do, I would have missed a tender opportunity to comfort, honor, and encourage my friend, who had done so many things in the past to serve me.

Even though I couldn't honor Vic by washing his feet, I could serve him by sitting at his side. I could show love with my prayers and tears.

There are stories you could tell about conferring status to those you love. Others may have to do with casual encounters you've had

> *As we learn to live the Jesus Experiment, I know we'll validate the promise of Jesus that he came to give us abundant life.*

at the gas station or grocery store, or in meetings. Unfortunately, most of us could tell about the times we let opportunities slip away, by cutting in line, vying for a position of honor, or preening like a peacock with the hope we'd be noticed. But as we learn to

live the Jesus Experiment, I know we'll validate the promise of Jesus that he came to give us abundant life. I can think of nothing that creates more joy than to love others as Jesus did—by serving and honoring them, not seeking to boost our own status. In a strange twist, we'll learn that when we serve, we are blessed; when we give respect, we are respected. As James, the half-brother of Jesus, said, "Humble yourselves before the Lord, and he will lift you up" (James 4:10).

Living the Jesus Experiment

This Week

When you encounter opportunities to honor, respect, and serve people who are seeking status, ask yourself what Jesus would feel, think, say, and do in the same situation. Now take note of your own responses. What are you feeling, thinking, saying, and doing? As you abide in Christ, ask God to help you honor and serve others as he would.

Ask

Read John 13:1-17. On the chart on page 190, examine the left-hand column, noting what Jesus felt, thought, said, and did as he dealt with the competitiveness of his disciples.

What does John 13:1-4 tell us about Jesus' mind-set as he approached his disciples and their time together?

_____

_____

_____

_____

Reread John 13:13-17. What are some lessons Jesus taught his disciples by washing their feet? What does this teach us about how we should treat other people who are competing for status?

_____

_____

_____

_____

Observe

Briefly describe a recent, specific situation in your life when you had an opportunity to give respect and status to someone, but didn't.

_____

_____

_____

_____

Fill in the center column of the chart (p. 190), recording how you felt, thought, spoke, and acted in that situation.

Evaluate

Prayerfully consider how you can begin to extend honor to other people, rather than seeking it. How can you give respect, rather than grabbing it?

_____

_____

_____

_____

How would abiding in Christ produce a greater willingness to serve people you know well? How about people you know casually? What about those you don't know?

_____

_____

_____

_____

Fill in the right-hand column of the chart, recording what you believe you would feel, think, say, and do about serving other people if you were abiding in Christ and following his example.

Apply

Think of the people in your life—at home, work, church, and in the community. What are some ways you can serve them in the coming week?

_____

_____

_____

_____

Write some specific steps you'll take to prepare yourself for the next time you have an opportunity to honor, respect, and serve someone who is seeking status. Spend a few minutes in prayer, asking God to guide you.

_____

_____

_____

_____

Here are a few ideas to get you started:

- Meditate on passages that reflect God's respect for you and how he values you for who you are (consider Psalm 139; John 3:16-20; Romans 12:1-8).
- Memorize a motivational verse from this passage or others that help you serve others and seize opportunities in Christ (consider Philippians 2:5-11).

One Week Later

Record your thoughts about how living the Jesus Experiment helped you respect, honor, and serve other people during the past seven days. How has abiding in Christ and following his example made your life more rich and satisfying?

_____

_____

_____

_____

_____

_____

REGARDING STATUS		
What did Jesus . . .	**What do I . . .**	
Feel? "Having loved his own who were in the world, he now showed them the full extent of his love." (John 13:1)	*Feel when self-reliant?*	*Feel when abiding in Jesus?*
Think? "Jesus knew that the Father had put all things under his power, and that he had come from God and was returning to God." (John 13:3)	*Think when self-reliant?*	*Think when abiding in Jesus?*
Say? "No servant is greater than his master, nor is a messenger greater than the one who sent him. Now that you know these things, you will be blessed if you do them." (John 13:16-17)	*Say when self-reliant?*	*Say when abiding in Jesus?*
Do? "He got up from the meal, took off his outer clothing, and wrapped a towel around his waist. After that, he poured water into a basin and began to wash his disciples' feet." (John 13:4-5)	*Do when self-reliant?*	*Do when abiding in Jesus?*

Download full-size charts and study questions at www.jesusexperiment.com.

He Gave Hope
to the Vulnerable

AS MY SON Ryan and I sat on a concrete pier overlooking the Ganges River in Varanasi, India, two men approached in a small wooden rowboat. Their taut faces made it clear they were angry. After tying the boat to the wooden landing below, they climbed the steps to the top of the pier and walked, barefoot, toward us.

"Stay here," our guide, a street kid named Raj, said as he walked quickly toward the men.

Smoke from street vendors cooking their food, ceremonial fires, burning piles of trash, cremated bodies, and incense wafted above the city in the cool morning air. A temple bell rang in the distance. On the other side of the river, a pack of dogs tore at a human body that had washed ashore.

Speaking in Hindi, the two men yelled at Raj in words that sounded like angry, discordant notes. Though I couldn't understand them, it didn't look good for our young friend.

Suddenly, with the sickening sound of fist on flesh, one of the men struck Raj on his left cheek. Before Raj could lift a hand in defense or run away, the other man delivered a second blow. Raj grabbed his face and bent over, cowering before his attackers.

I didn't know what to do. I feared defending Raj because the men might be armed or part of a gang. And we were foreigners.

Before we could intervene even if we had chosen to, the men turned and trotted away, their dirty work done.

I felt the relief of a coward whose fear remains unseen to everyone but himself.

"We must go see my uncle," Raj said, as he rubbed his red and swollen cheek. I had learned that, in India, "uncle" can refer to either a relative or a close male friend.

"Who's your uncle?" Ryan asked.

"He is the man who defends the lowest caste in Varanasi."

I felt the relief of a coward whose fear remains unseen to everyone but himself.

We followed Raj through a maze of streets only five or six feet wide, stepping gingerly around assorted trash, resting cows, and piles of cow dung on our way to his uncle's home. Once there, we walked up three flights of stairs to a shaded balcony on the roof, where our host offered us a cup of chai and a place to sit.

Raj and his uncle spoke for five or ten minutes before he asked us, in accented English, what had happened. After we told him, he thanked us and said, "I will take care of this."

Once on the street again, I asked Raj what his uncle would do.

"He will have them killed."

Ryan and I glanced at each other. All we had wanted was to help out a poor kid and see Varanasi through the eyes of a local. Now we were witnesses to a beating and the arrangement of a revenge killing.

The next morning, as the sun rose over the Ganges, Raj met us at the guarded gate of our riverfront hotel. He looked happy.

"The two men found out my uncle was going to have them killed, so they went to his home and apologized," he said. "They also apologized to me. Everything is fine."

As I reflect on that drama, I don't pretend to understand what happened and I'm not condoning a death threat to evoke an apology. But I am impressed that, in Varanasi, there is a man who protects the poorest of the poor . . . the weakest of the weak . . . the most vulnerable. There is someone kids like Raj can run to for help.

The Most Vulnerable

The downcast and weak likely felt the same way about Jesus. Not that he would use violence to protect them, but that he would stand up for them.

On the road to Jericho, when the crowds tried to silence two blind men crying out for help, Jesus stopped and healed them (Matthew 20:29-4). While dining in the home of a Pharisee, he defended a reputedly sinful woman who anointed his feet with her tears and expensive perfume (Luke 7:36-50). Another woman, caught in adultery, found safety in his words and forgiveness in his love (John 8:1-11).

On the road to Jericho, when the crowds tried to silence two blind men crying out for help, Jesus stopped and healed them.

After John the Baptist was thrown in jail, he sent messengers to Jesus with a question: "Are you the one who is to come, or should we expect someone else?"

Jesus told the messengers, "Go back and report to John what you have seen and heard: The blind receive sight, the lame walk, those who have leprosy are cured, the deaf hear, the dead are raised, and the good news is preached to the poor" (Luke 7:18-22). Jesus declared that his identity was proven by his ministry, not amongst the "powerful," but among the neediest of Israel.

If you read the Gospel accounts with an eye toward Jesus' treatment of the poor, sick, and downtrodden, you will discover he cared for the most vulnerable around him by seeing their greatest need and meeting it. And in doing so, he changed their lives.

The Jesus Experiment

It's easy to forget that women suffered under cultural, legal, and religious oppression in first-century Palestine. Jewish law marked women as inferior to men in all things, and they were often accorded the same status as "slaves and minors."[23] In the midst of this culture, Jesus always treated women with compassion and respect. He repeatedly violated cultural mores to reach out and care for women and other oppressed people.

The Samaritan woman Jesus met at a well was certainly an outcast. She had been through five marriages that had left her either a widow or a divorcée (John 4:18). No doubt, like many women, she had suffered deep wounds from hateful words and spiteful actions—not only from the men who had rejected her, but also from other women who condemned her lifestyle. Why else would she walk alone to Jacob's well under the scorching noonday sun? Typically, women drew water from a well nearer to town during the cool of the morning. I suspect she made the half-mile trek alone to avoid the indifference, insults, or glares of her female neighbors.

Jesus repeatedly violated cultural mores to reach out and care for women and other oppressed people.

As she approached the well, she saw a man—by his dress, a Jewish man—sitting beside the road watching her. Like a thief spotting the chief of police, she probably wished she wore an invisibility cloak. Without one, she likely lowered her head and went about dropping the leather bucket into the well.

One thing she knew for sure—there would be no conversation. Men did not speak with women in public. Rabbis never spoke with women. And Jews hated Samaritans. But Jesus was different.

What did Jesus feel and think?

It seems that Jesus' decision to route his trip through Samaria was a matter of convenience—at least from a human perspective. The threat of the religious Jews in Judea had prompted him to change the focus of his ministry from Judea to Galilee (John 4:1-42). Because Jesus neither hated nor feared the Samaritans, he took the shortest route to Galilee, which led through Samaria. When he arrived at the well after a twenty-mile hike, he sent his disciples into town for food (John 4:8). Though the Bible makes no mention of Jesus' emotional state, I think he felt sympathy for the woman arriving alone in the heat of the day. Clearly, she was troubled and alone, likely without friends; a woman who had suffered and who probably felt far from God. But she was closer than she realized, and Jesus was about to change her life.

Jesus didn't see the woman as a hated Samaritan to be shunned. He saw her as a human soul in need of rest . . . a woman in need of acceptance. I'm convinced that the moment he saw her approach, he knew his Father had arranged the meeting. Jesus knew she needed living water for her parched soul.

> *The moment Jesus saw the woman approach, he knew his Father had arranged the meeting. Jesus knew she needed living water for her parched soul.*

What did Jesus say and do?

In the midst of an awkward silence fueled by hundreds of years of cultural baggage and taboos, Jesus broke every man-made rule by asking a simple question: "Will you give me a drink?" (John 4:7).

His question may have hung in the air as the woman assessed the situation. She hadn't expected him to speak, hadn't even imagined it as a possibility. How could he so casually, and even carelessly, ignore the racial and religious barriers separating them? But instead of handing him a cup of water, she asked the obvious question: "How can you ask me for a drink?" (John 4:9).

HE GAVE RESPECT

I can't think of a more natural question for a thirsty man to ask someone with a bucket of cool, fresh well water. But in Jesus' day, his question expressed more than a desire for water. In asking for a drink, he honored the woman. No devout, self-respecting Jew would speak to a Samaritan woman, let alone drink water drawn by a Samaritan woman from a Samaritan well, served in a Samaritan cup. The Jews believed the woman, the well, the bucket, the cup, and the rope were all defiled, unclean, unworthy. Touching any of them would bring defilement and judgment.

His treatment of the woman reminds me of an interaction he had with a leper. In ancient Israel, lepers were not allowed to touch or be touched. They had to cover their mouths with a cloth and shout a warning, "Unclean!" The word caused others to flee for fear they would be defiled. The appearance of lepers and the stench of rotting flesh kept people not just physically distant, but relationally disengaged.

One day a man with an advanced case of leprosy approached Jesus (Mark 1:40-42). Areas of raw flesh, scabs, and white shining spots covered much of his body. An arm or leg may have rotted off, leaving a twisted stub.

How did Jesus respond? He did what probably nobody had done in years. He *touched* the leper. And then he healed him. I probably would have healed him first and then given him a side hug or fist bump, careful not to touch his skin. But Jesus knew the man's need for human touch and acceptance was more important than his need for physical healing.

I think Jesus saw the same need in the Samaritan woman. The Lord's request told her, "You are not defiled, and you cannot defile me. I will speak with you. I will acknowledge your existence. I will let you satisfy my basic, human needs by drinking the water you offer me. I will drink it in your cup. You, a Samaritan outcast, are a person of dignity and worth." Jesus gave her the respect she needed. The kind needed by every disabled woman, homeless man, fatherless child, AIDS victim, and ex-con.

Jesus knew the man's need for human touch and acceptance was more important than his need for physical healing.

Sensing her discomfort, he said, perhaps with a smile, "If you knew the gift of God and who it is that asks you for a drink, you would have asked him and he would have given you living water" (John 4:10).

HE GAVE HOPE

If his initial request bolstered her confidence and piqued her curiosity, this statement confounded her. I don't think she could have been more skeptical if Jesus had said he wanted to give her a talking camel.

To the people of that region, Jews and Samaritans alike, "living water" was running water and was much preferred over well water—just as we might prefer filtered water over tap water. To this woman's ears, Jesus seemed to offer an endless supply of running water. If so, she would no longer have to make the daily trek to the well. But as she began considering his question, a couple of doubts surfaced.

First, how would he draw the water? Taking Jesus literally, she asked where he was going to get this water, since he had no bucket.

Second, who was this man deigning to speak with her? With

that second question, she felt a flicker of hope. She asked, "Are you greater than our father, Jacob, who gave us the well and drank from it himself, as did also his sons and his flocks and herds?" (John 4:12).

Jacob's well provided water that temporarily quenched a person's thirst. The water Jesus offered would quench her thirst forever.

The woman realized Jesus was implying something remarkable—that he was greater than Jacob.

Instead of giving a yes or no answer, Jesus clarified what he meant by "living water." He said that Jacob's well provided water that temporarily quenched a person's thirst. The water he offered would quench her thirst forever (John 4:14).

Hope drove her to seek more from Jesus. "Sir, give me this water so that I won't get thirsty and have to keep coming here to draw water" (John 4:15).

Though Jesus was willing to fulfill her request, he first wanted her to recognize her true need. So he said, "Go, call your husband and come back." On the surface, it might have seemed a reasonable request. After all, according to social custom, Jesus shouldn't have been talking to the woman at all. With that simple request, though, he revealed the woman's secret life.

HE PROVED TRUSTWORTHY

"I have no husband," the woman said, probably blushing in shame.

In response, Jesus spoke the painful truth, gently exposing a reality she had concealed. "You are right when you say you have no husband. The fact is, you have had five husbands, and the man you now have is not your husband. What you have just said is quite true" (John 4:17-18).

While putting his finger on the undiluted reality of the woman's life, Jesus also *praised* her for telling the truth. Somehow, he had pulled from her brief admission the very thing she was using the truth to hide.

After his startling statement, she said, "I can see that you are a prophet. Our ancestors worshiped on this mountain, but you Jews claim that the place where we must worship is in Jerusalem." The mountain she referred to, and likely gestured toward, was Mt. Gerizim, where the Samaritans had built their temple.

With his next comment, Jesus could have wounded her spirit and shut her down. Yet for her to find God, he knew the woman needed to hear his words. So he spoke, truthfully and directly, exposing the fallacy of her belief system. He told her the Samaritans worshiped in ignorance and the Jews in knowledge, for "salvation is from the Jews" (John 4:21-24).

Instead of defending her religion or heritage, she said, "'I know that Messiah' (called Christ) 'is coming. When he comes, he will explain everything to us'" (John 4:25).

Jesus then spoke the ultimate truth: "I who speak to you am he" (John 4:26).

By the time Jesus made this statement, the woman had learned to trust him. He had respectfully accepted her without judgment. He had offered the hope of eternal life. He had gently spoken the truth about her shameful past and praised her character. And in her heart, she knew he had also spoken the truth about himself.

Jesus then spoke the ultimate truth: "I who speak to you am he."

When the disciples returned from their food run, the woman walked back to town with amazing news, "Come, see a man who told me everything I ever did. Could this be the Christ?" (John 4:29).

In light of her five marriages, it's no wonder that statement grabbed everyone's attention. Of course, the word *everything* could involve a lot more than her five husbands. When she returned to the well, the villagers formed a parade behind her.

For two days, the Samaritans listened to Jesus. Because he interacted graciously and truthfully with a woman who was among the town's most vulnerable, she not only believed, she brought a village with her (John 4:28-42).

What I feel and think

There are opportunities all around us to help vulnerable people. But we have to be alert or we could miss them. That almost happened to me.

I'm not much for long drives, but when a friend in Illinois gave me a car, I was pretty excited about driving it home to Portland. After speaking at a men's event in Rockford, I picked up the car in Chicago and headed to Denver to visit my friend Jeff, who was battling cancer at the time, and pick up my son Ryan, who had agreed to accompany me on the Denver-to-Portland leg.

There are opportunities all around us to help vulnerable people. But we have to be alert or we could miss them.

After driving several hours, I exited the freeway to get gas. While fueling the car, I noticed the front tires looked low on air. Just about that time, the skillet-gray sky split open, sending down a barrage of pea-sized raindrops. Because the air pump was out in the open, I decided to hit the road and fill the tires after the rain let up.

Thirty minutes later, God turned off the water spigot and I exited the freeway again. At a traffic light just off the Interstate, I saw a young couple trying to hitch a ride on the on-ramp. Normally, I wouldn't give hitchhikers a second thought. Everyone knows it's dangerous to pick up strangers. But writing about how Jesus helped the vulnerable caused me to see them as people without a car, not bandits.

Were they vulnerable? It seemed that way to me. After all, they were at the mercy of anyone who picked them up. While overfilling the tires, because I had no gauge and was guessing at the pressure, I decided I would give them a ride if they were college students.

What I say and do

It turned out they attended the University of Chicago and were going to Denver for spring break. Will was a political science major from Boston, and Sarah was a talkative philosophy student from New York City. It had taken them six rides to travel one hundred miles. They had camped near the freeway the night before and had just about given up hope of another ride when I came along. They were so excited when I agreed to drive them all the way to Denver, they would have blown party whistles if they'd had them.

Will said they were "lucky" I came along. I told him I thought it was "divine providence." I had stopped twenty miles back to get gas, and if it hadn't been raining, I wouldn't have gotten off the freeway again to get air in the tires. I'm convinced God orchestrated the events so I could drive them safely to Denver. Several friends told me I had taken a risk. I told them I felt comfortable with Jesus at my side. I couldn't remember fear keeping Jesus from helping someone in need.

We talked about a lot of subjects, and somewhere in the conversation Will asked why I had picked them up. I told him it had to do with an experiment I was living: the Jesus Experiment. I explained how Jesus helped vulnerable people in need and how I thought if he were driving my car, he would have picked them up. So I did.

SEEKING THE VULNERABLE

Of course, helping vulnerable people should not merely be something we do when it's convenient. Like Jesus traveling to the well and spending two days in Samaria, we ought to seek out the vulnerable and invest in their lives.

Like my middle son, David. Last year, he moved to Thailand to teach English as a second language. Once there, he found a job teaching children orphaned by the 2004 tsunami. Five days a week, he pours his life into vulnerable kids.

Closer to home, my youngest son, Paul, recently moved to Jackson, Mississippi, for a year-long clerkship with a federal judge. After work one night, he went to a Switchfoot concert, where he heard John M. Perkins, a black civil rights leader, challenge the audience to get involved in the community by mentoring kids. Sensing a stirring in his soul, Paul decided to do it. Now, once a week, he leaves work during his lunch hour and drives to the west side of Jackson, a part of town most people have abandoned, to invest in the lives of three fifth-grade boys who come from broken families with an absent, or unknown, father. The boys have slowly, and sometimes suddenly, opened up about their hurts and fears and their hopes and dreams. Paul sees serving these boys as part of the reason God called him to Jackson.

Like Jesus traveling to the well and spending two days in Samaria, we ought to seek out the vulnerable and invest in their lives.

One of the most touching stories I've heard about someone going out of her way to help vulnerable children involved my friend Mona.

MONA'S STORY

I met Mona ten years ago. She's tall, five feet eleven inches, with a quick smile and a contagious laugh. When I first met her, she had already endured scores of surgeries to repair damage done during a car wreck.

The accident occurred on Thanksgiving Day, 1982. After dinner with her family, Mona and three friends hopped in a car and headed back to college. On a good-weather day, the trip would have been a breeze. But it was a bad-weather day, and sleet had glazed a bridge they were crossing. The driver lost control of the car, hit another vehicle, and slid into the concrete siding. The gas cap came off, spewing fuel on Mona as she was hurled from the car. A spark ignited her coat, enveloping her with flames and charring her face and hands.

Years later, Mona felt compelled to reach out to a young burn victim on the other side of the world.

I asked Mona if she would write something about Sonia, the girl she met in a Russian hospital.

> *Bill, you asked what motivated me to help Sonia. Yes, it was unexpected. When I first went to the burn center in Volgograd, I didn't know if they would let me step foot in the place. Most burn centers are closed to all visitors, and strangers are more than frowned upon in Russia.*
>
> *Being a burn survivor helped pave the way. That Thanksgiving inferno left me with a lost identity, limited hand function, and more scars than a young woman should ever have to deal with.*
>
> *It took thirty surgeries and a lot of soul-searching over the next decade to piece some kind of identity back together. God's love kept me sane and holding on to hope, though the why? question haunted me. The drive to make some sense out of my own injury led me to reach out to other survivors. There is camaraderie among us, a shared reality.*
>
> *Maybe the director of the burn center understood that when he looked at me, or maybe he saw dollars, but he gave me access. Finding a sweet ten-year-old orphaned girl all alone and in great pain was wrenching. I felt helpless but quickly figured out that any time I could spend at her bedside infused her with hope and comfort.*

My interpreter and I struggled to find the time to travel across town to be with Sonia amidst a busy team schedule, but she became very dear to us.

The docs didn't give her much hope for survival. The grafts they tried to give her didn't take, but she fought on and on. Days turned into weeks, and weeks into months. We didn't know from day to day if she would still be alive when we arrived. She surprised everyone and rallied time and time again. The ups and downs and twists and turns tore at us. For Sonia, nothing mattered but living one more day.

How can I describe this little girl? She was cute, tenacious, and very brave. She would sing through pain-filled days, crack jokes, and lure everyone into her sweet little web. But sadly, she had few real advocates. We pushed for antibiotics and pain meds, scarce resources reserved for patients who had bribes to give, a fact hidden from me at the time.

How can I describe her suffering? Sonia had festering wounds, covering most of her body, that needed to be treated. They had to anesthetize her to even touch her bandages. I've never encountered anything like it before or since. It was a roller coaster of one day asking God for her life and the next pleading for her death.

Sonia lived seven long months before her little heart gave out. I had been praying that I could be there at the end, but she passed early one spring morning with no loved ones surrounding her. Knowing the Great Advocate was waiting on the other side consoled my heart.

You don't walk away from the Sonias of the world unscathed or unchanged. She fostered a small crusade in my heart to reach out to others like her.

The thing about compassion is that it can take you through

dark, unexpected waters. Your reaching out may not divert the disaster, but it might mitigate some of the effects.

I told her stories. I held her hand. I shared her journey.

Despite the trauma, there were moments of connection, seconds of joy.

I was in no way adequate for the task, but I believed that God would take my meager offering and use it to feed one of His precious souls. I believe Jesus had lived and loved through me.

As you abide in Jesus and live the Jesus Experiment, seeking to serve and love the vulnerable of this world, he will do the same through you.

Living the Jesus Experiment

This Week

It's unlikely a vulnerable person will knock on your door this week and ask for help. Jesus went to Samaria, spoke with the woman at the well, and then invested two days with her and the rest of her village. Take some time this week to identify someone you (or your small group) could help. Remember, this might require you to go out of your way or sacrifice time you might not want to give. But this is what we're called to do; this is Jesus' example we are called to follow.

As you consider this, ask yourself what Jesus would feel, think, say, and do in the same situation. Now take note of your own responses. What are you feeling, thinking, saying, and doing? As you abide in Jesus this week, ask God to prompt you to take the necessary steps to find and help someone in need.

Ask

Read John 4:4-42. On the chart on page 209, examine the left-hand column, noting what Jesus felt, thought, said, and did in his encounter with a vulnerable person.

How much effort did Jesus expend in talking with the woman at the well?

_____

_____

_____

_____

How did Jesus show respect and create hope in the context of truth for the Samaritan woman?

_____

_____

_____

_____

Observe

Briefly describe a recent, specific situation in your life when you allowed bias and prejudice to affect how you treated a vulnerable person.

_____

_____

_____

_____

Fill in the center column of the chart (p. 209), recording how you felt, thought, spoke, and acted when you were judgmental and self-reliant.

Evaluate

Fill in the right-hand column of the chart, recording how you believe you would feel, think, speak, and act in that same situation if you were abiding in Jesus and following his example.

Apply

Write some specific steps you will take to find and help a vulnerable person. This exercise is going to take some effort on your part, but it will be more than worth it. Spend a few minutes in prayer, asking God to guide you.

_____

_____

_____

Here are a few ideas to get you started:

- Memorize a motivational verse that helps you treat vulnerable people as Jesus would. You might consider James 1:27: "Religion that God our Father accepts as pure and faultless is this: to look after orphans and widows in their distress and to keep oneself from being polluted by the world."
- Discuss some of the insights into your biases and prejudices with a friend or small group, and give someone permission to ask you questions about how you will seek to help someone in need.
- Journal about your interactions with vulnerable people and pray for God's grace and strength to continue to live the Jesus Experiment in these relationships.
- Identify a way you could find and help someone in need. Specify when and how you will extend the love of Christ to that person.

If you'd like some help identifying vulnerable people in your area, please check out the following resources:

- Author Donald Miller has a boys' mentoring organization called The Mentoring Project: www.thementoringproject.org.
- AmeriCorps is a government organization that connects the public with all types of volunteer opportunities: www .americorps.gov.
- Points of Light Institute is President George H.W. Bush's volunteer organization, which connects people to service opportunities: www.pointsoflight.org.
- If you'd like to help rescue children in developing countries, go to www.lifesongfororphans.org.
- The New Commandment ministry connects men in a church with single parents, widows, and the disabled. The men commit a few hours one day a month to meet long-term needs: www.newcommandment.org.

One Week Later

Record your thoughts about how living the Jesus Experiment helped you give hope and worth to a vulnerable person during the past seven days. How did abiding in Christ and following his example make your life more rich and satisfying as you helped someone in need?

_____

_____

_____

_____

_____

_____

_____

REGARDING VULNERABLE PEOPLE

What did Jesus . . .	What do I . . .	
Feel? Possibly, Jesus felt sympathy for the woman alone at the well in the heat of the day. In admitting his physical thirst (John 4:7), Jesus identified with our human weakness.	*Feel when self-reliant?*	*Feel when abiding in Jesus?*
Think? Jesus thought it was proper to associate with Samaritans, unlike most Jews at the time. (John 4:9) That this woman needed acceptance and living water. (John 4:10-11)	*Think when self-reliant?*	*Think when abiding in Jesus?*
Say? "Will you give me a drink?" (John 4:7) "If you knew the gift of God and who it is that asks you for a drink, you would have asked him and he would have given you living water." (John 4:10) "The water I give them will become in them a spring of water welling up to eternal life." (John 4:14)	*Say when self-reliant?*	*Say when abiding in Jesus?*
Do? He sat down by the well. (John 4:6) He engaged in conversation with the woman. (John 4:7-26) He instructed the disciples. (John 4:32-38) When the Samaritans urged him to stay with them, he stayed two days. (John 4:40)	*Do when self-reliant?*	*Do when abiding in Jesus?*

Download full-size charts and study questions at www.jesusexperiment.com.

He Blessed Children

"WHERE DID ALL these people come from?" I asked Cindy. Stretching before us was a jam-packed parking lot that offered few open spaces. Meanwhile, a hundred kids kicked soccer balls across three fields as their parents watched, shouted, and took pictures.

Why had I never noticed this great social gathering? As I contemplated the question, I realized I *had* noticed. I'd just never given it a second thought. I had driven past Little League fields boasting bleachers packed with screaming parents. I had seen kids chasing a soccer ball as their parents cheered from the sidelines. But with my kids too young to play, I paid it no more attention than I would the score of an Australian cricket match.

The year Ryan turned six, everything changed, and the Great Sports Vortex pulled me in as it has millions of other parents.

From late summer until early winter, soccer season takes over households across Oregon. Every Saturday, from nine in the morning until three in the afternoon, hordes of vehicles bearing enthusiastic, caffeine-buzzed parents and adrenaline-pumped kids migrate to the athletic fields.

That's what brought me to the crowded sideline of a soccer field one cool September morning.

Shortly after the whistle blew for Ryan's first game, I noticed something was wrong. My freckle-faced boy remained on the sidelines like a dejected puppy, picking at the grass while his teammates scurried around the ball like a herd of squirrels, yelling and kicking the air. The scene saddened, angered, and bored me.

When the referee whistled a time-out for substitutions, Ryan dropped a fistful of grass and trotted onto the field. For me, it was as if a spotlight from heaven flickered on, with Ryan in the center of its beam. Boredom evolved into excitement, and the game of soccer hooked me. Over the next eleven years, I coached all three of my sons in a sport I hadn't played.

After I had coached Ryan for a few years, David started playing. So I signed up to coach his team. After a few weeks, I realized what had worked with Ryan didn't work with David. I could teach Ryan a few moves, and he'd practice alone for hours. With David, I couldn't bribe him to practice alone. A few years later, when I began coaching Paul's team, I discovered I had to develop a new strategy with him as well. Not only did I have to teach Paul what to practice, but I had to *explain* the benefits of practicing alone.

We must adapt our approach—as parents, teachers, coaches, and friends—to a child's personality.

Every parent who has more than one child eventually comes to the same realization: Each child is unique. What works with one fails with another. That's why we must adapt our approach—as parents, teachers, coaches, and friends—to a child's personality.

Solomon says as much when he writes, "Train a child in the way he should go, and when he is old he will not turn from it" (Proverbs 22:6). The word for "way" is used elsewhere by Solomon to refer to "the way of an eagle in the sky . . . a snake on a rock . . . a ship on the high seas, and . . . a man with a maiden" (Proverbs 30:18-19). Each of those four wonders enjoys a special beauty, something almost mysterious.

A child's "way" isn't a well-defined path. It's a unique set of characteristics that sets him or her apart.

That Old Testament sage urged us to value every child's unique traits and characteristics. He wanted our interactions with children to harmonize with their uniqueness. But how do we do that?

> *A child's "way" isn't a well-defined path. It's a unique set of characteristics that sets him or her apart.*

The Jesus Experiment

What did Jesus feel and think?

As Jesus walked through Judea, crowds pressed in on him. Working their way through the horde, parents asked Jesus to lay hands on their children and bless them. The disciples, annoyed by the brashness of these mothers and fathers, offered harsh rebukes.

When Jesus saw the disciples stiff-arm the parents, he became indignant. He told them, "Let the little children come to me, and do not hinder them, for the kingdom of God belongs to such as these. I tell you the truth, anyone who will not receive the kingdom of God like a little child will never enter it" (Mark 10:13-15).

Jesus felt it was his responsibility to protect children.

It's interesting the Bible tells us Jesus was "indignant." The word speaks of anger aroused by something unjust or mean.[24] This may have been because the disciples had been especially harsh with the parents. The truth is, Jesus didn't view children as inferior people undeserving of his attention. Indeed, he used their trust in God as an example of undiluted and wholehearted faith, the kind everyone must possess to enter God's kingdom.

What I feel and think

Before the birth of our first son, I feared I wouldn't like him. My concern was rooted in a childhood experience. When I was seven, my eldest sister had a baby; and when she brought him home, she asked if I wanted to hold him. I told her I did.

As she held him out for me to take, she issued a warning: "His neck muscles aren't strong yet, so you have to support his head with your hand, or his head will fall to the side. His neck could break, killing or paralyzing him."

Jesus didn't view children as inferior people undeserving of his attention. Indeed, he used their trust in God as an example of undiluted and wholehearted faith.

I swallowed hard and reached for the infant. But my sister gave another warning. "The bones on his head haven't grown together yet, and if you jab your thumb into the soft spot on top of his head, it will squish into his brain, killing or paralyzing him. Do you want to hold him?"

By then I was terrified I might injure or kill my newborn nephew. But I felt an obligation to hold him, so I nodded my head and said, "Sure, I'll hold him."

Like a child contortionist, I twisted my wrist, hand, and arm so I could cradle his body and support his head. Curious about the no-touch zone on his head, I gently pushed my index finger into the soft spot. Sure enough, it was as pliable as a wet sponge. Though my gentle touch didn't kill or paralyze him, at about the same instant, the little tyke erupted with a geyser of cottage cheese–like liquid from one end and a flow of funny-smelling chocolate milk from the other. With my T-shirt now a brown-and-white tie-dye, I handed the screaming infant back to my sister.

It's funny how that experience seared my brain with an apprehension about children that wasn't overcome until my first son entered the world. After his birth, I quickly learned that children are a bundle of love and laughter, even though they do make messes.

I enjoy children and feel compassion for those who suffer. There have been occasions, though, when I've rushed past needy children with no more than a wave. Sometimes, when I'm working or in a hurry, I've *Jesus always took time for people— especially children—and he blessed them.* viewed them as an intrusion. I'm sure Jesus never did. He always took time for people—especially children—and he blessed them.

What did Jesus say and do?

After I visited a slum in Vishakhapatnam, a modern city on the Bay of Bengal, my guide, the founder of a handful of orphanages, offered me a sanitary wipe for my hands.

"The children are filthy," he said. "You must clean your hands."

As I took one of the white wipes, I noticed he hadn't used one himself. "Don't you need one?" I asked.

"Oh, I never touch the children," he said. "Never! They're too dirty."

Like a slap across the cheek, his words stunned me. How could he love children and not display affection?

Maybe that's the kind of disregard Jesus saw in his disciples. We can't know exactly, but what we do know is Jesus showed no such indifference. Mark notes, "He took the children in his arms, put his hands on them and blessed them" (Mark 10:16). In those days, "to bless" meant "to speak well of" or "praise" someone. In Old Testament times, a blessing transferred a good thing from one person to another. When Isaac, under God's direction, blessed Jacob, he imparted the promise of bountiful crops, many servants, and leadership in the family (Genesis 27:27-29). Blessings were important, and more than just a passing prayer.

It's impossible to overstate the value of speaking uplifting words to children.

Though we don't have the ability to give a blessing with similar benefits, we can pass on valuable gifts to children, such as a sense of security and destiny.

Jesus opened his mouth and spoke a blessing to the children gathered around him. Years before, Abraham had spoken a blessing to Isaac, Isaac had uttered a blessing to Jacob, and Jacob had spoken a blessing to his twelve sons and two grandchildren.

HEALTHY WORDS

It's impossible to overstate the value of speaking uplifting words to children. A study of maladjusted students in a large Oklahoma high school revealed the importance of verbal affirmation.

The counselors in the school first developed close relationships with ten of the school's most troubled teens. Next, the counselors asked, "How long has it been since your parents told you they loved you?" Only one of the students could remember hearing those words, and even he couldn't remember when it happened.

In sharp contrast, when students considered well-adjusted were asked the same question, their responses were often "this morning," "last evening," or "yesterday."[25] In Proverbs 25:11, Solomon highlights the importance of kind words spoken at the right moment: "A word aptly spoken is like apples of gold in settings of silver." Our words should fit the needs of a child as snugly as an apple of gold fits a ring's silver setting.

When I've made this point while speaking, occasionally a parent or two will call me aside to explain (read: rationalize) their unique situation. These parents know they are critical of their children, but claim it's because the kids seldom do anything right.

I remind them it's a matter of focus. A wart on the nose isn't pretty, but it's not the child's entire face. If the warts become the parents' focus, they may begin to think of their children as frogs. Unconsciously affected by how their parents view them, the kids may come to see themselves as frogs.

I remember when my youngest son, Paul, played Little League baseball. Because he was the fastest boy on the team, he started the season as the leadoff hitter. After seven games, though, he hadn't gotten a hit and was moved to the bottom of the batting order. Every game, I sat behind the backstop and encouraged him. "Good swing. Great form. Nice try." The thing is, Paul had a great swing, and he could hit the ball far when he made contact. He just couldn't connect. To help him, we started practicing in the backyard with golf-size Wiffle balls.

Solomon highlights the importance of kind words spoken at the right moment: "A word aptly spoken is like apples of gold in settings of silver."

A couple of games later, he finally broke out of his hitting slump, rocketing a ball between the shortstop and second baseman into center field. As Paul rounded first base and made it to second, I don't doubt the coach remembered why he had wanted him to bat leadoff. His next time up, he hit another double, and then a single. After that game, Paul returned to his spot as leadoff hitter.

During Paul's hitting slump I was tempted to focus on the negative. Yet I've never met a child who needed to be reminded of his failures. Children crave words of blessing and affirmation. They need adults to focus on the positive. We shouldn't ignore the bad, but we should *concentrate* on the positive.

A mother once told me she was afraid that if she praised her daughter all the time, the girl would become arrogant. I told her she could avoid that by not comparing her daughter to other girls. It also helps to praise good attitudes and hard work, rather than positive results, such as good grades or the number of goals scored in a soccer game. If we affirm our children's attitudes, they will feel good about themselves whether they're straight-A students or not. If they've done their best, that's praiseworthy.

If we affirm our children's attitudes, they will feel good about themselves whether they're straight-A students or not.

When our boys were young, we made it a habit to hold them every night, look into their eyes, and say, "I'll love you forever, no matter what." Now that they're grown, I can tell you there were more than a few "no matter whats." Though our sons are now scattered across the globe, we try to talk with them daily—although that's hard with the one who lives in Asia. In every conversation, we want them to know we believe in them and love them.

Don't wait to bless your children. Don't think, *They already know I appreciate them. I don't need to say it again.* Jesus didn't hold back a blessing from a child. He knew that a blessing isn't a blessing until it's spoken.

HEALTHY HUGS

Jesus didn't loom over the kids and deliver a stern lecture. He blessed them not only verbally, but physically. He gathered them into his arms and hugged them. He laid his calloused hands on their shoulders, making rejected children feel loved.

One day, Jesus visited Peter's sick mother-in-law and healed her with a touch of his hand. On the Mount of Transfiguration, when Jesus pulled back the cloak of his humanity and allowed his divinity to shine through, the disciples fell to the ground terrified. Jesus touched them and told them not to fear.

Why did Jesus so frequently reach out his hands to touch hurting people? He could have healed the blind man, or Peter's mother-in-law, with a word. He could have commanded his disciples not to fear without bending down to touch them. Jesus touched people because he knew the immense human craving for love and acceptance.

We live in a nation of children who are emotionally malnourished because, in part, they are starved for affection. Unfortunately, many studies indicate most parents only touch their children when necessity demands. Parents usually only touch their children when helping them dress, undress, or get into a car.[26] Yet affectionate physical contact is crucial to the emotional development of boys and girls.[27]

Jesus touched people because he knew the immense human craving for love and acceptance.

Psychologist Harry Harlow conducted a set of experiments during the 1950s that showed the importance of a tender touch. He separated infant monkeys from their mothers a few hours after birth, then arranged for the young animals to be "raised" by two kinds of surrogates, either of which could be equipped to dispense milk. One surrogate mother was made of bare-wire mesh; the other was covered with soft terry cloth. Harlow first observed that monkeys with a choice of mothers spent far more time clinging to the terry-cloth surrogates, even when their physical nourishment came from bottles mounted on the bare-wire mothers.

Harlow found that when he separated the infants into two groups and gave them no choice between the two types of mothers, all drank equally and grew physically at the same rate. But those with the soft, tactile contact with their terry-cloth mother behaved differently than those whose mother was made of cold, hard wire. When frightened, the babies with a terry-cloth mother made bodily contact with her, rubbed against her, and calmed down. After their initial fright subsided, they remained playful and curious. Those with the wire-mesh mother threw themselves on the floor, clutched themselves, rocked back and forth, and screamed in terror.[28]

God is not a wire-mesh surrogate. He's not even a terry-cloth God. He took on the full form of warm, human flesh, with arms and hands that touched and hugged. The need for adult affection is immense among children. I'm convinced that children who receive appropriate hugs and touches from their parents will be able to recognize inappropriate touching. I also believe they are far less likely as teens to act out on cravings for sexual intimacy.

God is not a wire-mesh surrogate. He's not even a terry-cloth God. He took on the full form of warm, human flesh, with arms and hands that touched and hugged.

When my sons were young, I had a blast wrestling with them—one at a time or three-on-one against me. I once asked my youngest son how he knew I loved him. He thought for a moment and then said, "Because you wrestle with me." Now that they're men, I always greet them with a bear hug and a kiss on the cheek.

Touching is simple. A gentle poke in the ribs, a ruffling of the hair, a hug, a hand on the shoulder. These affectionate acts give children a sense of belonging, well-being, and security.

But even that's not enough. There is one more thing I believe Jesus did when he blessed children. It's also something we must do.

HEALTHY PREDICTIONS

The biblical concept of a blessing involved speaking words about the future of the person being blessed. When God first spoke to Abraham, he promised to give him land, many descendants, and a special heir through whom the world would be blessed (Genesis 12:1-3). Later, God promised Isaac a future to look forward to (Genesis 26:24). A generation later, God appeared to Jacob and promised the land upon which he slept (Genesis 28:1-13). Throughout the Bible, God reminds his children of their future.

Jesus stretched the imagination of his disciples with predictions about their future. He promised they would one day sit on thrones, judging the twelve tribes of Israel (Matthew 19:28). During the last supper, Jesus said he was going to prepare a place for them in his Father's house (John 14:2).

> *Jesus stretched the imagination of his disciples with predictions about their future.*

God's promises aren't confined to biblical characters. He also gives a wonderful picture of our future: "When he appears, we shall be like him, for we shall see him as he is" (1 John 3:2).

What I say and do

In our relationships with our children, we can't make predictions like God made of Abraham, Isaac, and Jacob. Nor can we speak with the confidence John had when he referred to our destiny as believers. But we can know our children well enough to imagine what God will accomplish through them.

When people read the dedication of my book *Six Battles Every Man Must Win*, they're initially shocked because I've dedicated it to my *favorite* son. But as they read the entire page, they discover I dedicated the book to each of my sons.

As I tucked my boys into bed when they were children, I said a prayer that expressed how I thought God would use them in the future. Amazingly, much of what I prayed has come to fruition.

My sons all have battles they've fought and won, and some they've fought and lost. But win or lose, they all believe God has a unique purpose for their lives.

If you are a parent or grandparent, ask God to give you insight into your children or grandchildren so you can affirm their future with encouraging predictions of how you believe God will use them. If you don't have children of your own, go out of your way to extend the love of Jesus to the children you encounter.

Ask God to give you insight into your children or grandchildren so you can affirm their future with encouraging predictions of how you believe God will use them.

A CHRISTMAS STORY

Snowflakes floated down from the cold, gray sky, painting the street and sidewalk white. It was Christmas Eve in London, 1940. The German bombings had been pounding the city for months, and more than a million homes were destroyed or damaged. A five-year-old boy, whose parents had been killed a few weeks before, pressed his nose against the window of a bakery, his breath fogging the glass. Inside, the baker pulled a tray of steaming hot cinnamon rolls from an oven.

A man walked behind the boy and entered the store. He spoke with the baker, who placed ten cinnamon rolls in one sack and two in another. After paying, the man opened the door and stepped outside. Tapping the boy's shoulder, he asked, "Would you like a cinnamon roll?"

"Yes, sir. I sure would," the boy said, his eyes filled with excitement.

The man handed him the sack with two rolls, patted him on the head, and turned to leave.

A moment later, the man felt something tugging on the tail of his coat. He turned around, looked down, and saw the wide-eyed boy looking up at him.

"Mister," the boy said. "Are you Jesus?"

Remember: We're never more like Jesus than when we care for a child.

Living the Jesus Experiment

This Week

Whenever you encounter a child, ask yourself what Jesus would feel, think, say, and do in the same situation. Now take note of your own responses. What are you feeling, thinking, saying, and doing? Pray that, as you abide in Christ, you will bless the children you encounter.

Ask

Read Mark 10:13-16. On the chart on page 226, examine the left-hand column, noting what Jesus felt, thought, said, and did in his encounters with children.

How did Jesus show love to the children?

_____

_____

Observe

Briefly describe a recent, specific situation in which you disregarded children or treated them as inferior. Note an instance or two where you honored a child and made him or her feel special.

_____

_____

_____

_____

_____

Fill in the center column of the chart (p. 226), recording how you felt, thought, spoke, and acted toward children when your focus was on yourself.

Evaluate

Who are some of the children you interact with most frequently? List their names and describe some of their unique characteristics and positive attributes.

_____

_____

_____

_____

_____

Fill in the right-hand column of the chart, recording what you believe you would feel, think, say, and do in that same situation if you were abiding in Jesus and following his example with children.

Apply

Read Genesis 27:27-29 and identify the elements of Isaac's blessing of Jacob. Now take your observations of the children in your life and turn those into blessings for them. You may want to use a piece of stationery to write out your blessing so you can give it to the children.

If you have children, be sure to give them healthy hugs and words of affirmation this week.

Write some specific steps that will help you become a frequent source of blessing for the children in your life as you depend on Jesus. Spend a few minutes in prayer, asking God to guide you.

_____

_____

_____

_____

_____

Here are a few ideas to get you started:

- Plan a regular date with each of your children and make part of the time together a special blessing by reflecting on their recent positive actions and the traits you see developing in them.
- Memorize Mark 10:16 and ask God to use it to help you follow the example of Jesus. "And he took the children in his arms, placed his hands on them and blessed them."
- Discuss with a friend or small group some of the insights into your barriers to blessing children. Give someone permission to ask you questions about your blessing of children.
- Spend a few minutes each day reflecting on your interactions with children, and ask God to help you become a vessel of blessing for the children in your life.

One Week Later

Record your thoughts about how abiding in Jesus and living the Jesus Experiment over the last seven days helped you treat children like Jesus did. How has blessing children as Jesus did made your life more abundant?

_____

_____

_____

_____

_____

_____

_____

_____

_____

_____

REGARDING CHILDREN

What did Jesus . . .	What do I . . .	
Feel? People were bringing little children to Jesus for him to place his hands on them, but the disciples rebuked them. When Jesus saw this, he was indignant. (Mark 10:13-14)	*Feel when self-reliant?*	*Feel when abiding in Jesus?*
Think? Jesus didn't view children as inferior people undeserving of his attention. He saw their trust in God as an example of undiluted, wholehearted faith.	*Think when self-reliant?*	*Think when abiding in Jesus?*
Say? "Let the little children come to me, and do not hinder them, for the kingdom of God belongs to such as these. I tell you the truth, anyone who will not receive the kingdom of God like a little child will never enter it." (Mark 10:14-15)	*Say when self-reliant?*	*Say when abiding in Jesus?*
Do? "He took the children in his arms, placed his hands on them and blessed them." (Mark 10:16)	*Do when self-reliant?*	*Do when abiding in Jesus?*

Download full-size charts and study questions at www.jesusexperiment.com.

He Loved Difficult People

OUR FAMILY USED to have a black Great Dane we affectionately named Big. When we got him, he was a tiny twenty-five pounds with lion-sized paws. Full grown, he tipped the scales at 185. One day, my son Paul took Big to school for show-and-tell. Later at soccer practice, Big grabbed the ball in his massive mouth and cantered around the field, chased by fifteen hollering kids.

The gentle colossus always attracted attention. During a soccer game, a woman approached me and said, "Wow! He's big. What's his name?"

"He's Big," I said.

"Yeah, I know. But what's his name?"

"Big," I repeated.

She laughed, patting the top of his massive head without knowing I had given him that name in anticipation of just such a question.

Though Big was a fun dog, he was also difficult. Because his head was countertop-high, no food was safe in the kitchen unless fiercely guarded. He could scoop a loaf of bread off the top of the refrigerator and wolf it down in seconds. When eating a snack, the boys had to walk with it held above their heads. The moment they lowered a hand, Big would nab their treats.

The Great Dane also had a problem with running away. If the front door was left open, he would sneak out and wander for miles. At first, we spent hours looking for him, but we quickly discovered nobody wanted to steal a dog his size. Where would they hide him? And who would want to pay his food and vet bills? And how many people own a mini front-end loader for waste removal?

We quickly discovered nobody wanted to steal a dog his size. Where would they hide him?

We eventually got to the point where, if we didn't find him on a quick drive around the block, we'd call the police. Without exception, someone had reported a huge dog hanging around his house or lying in her front yard. I'd drive to the designated house, honk the horn, and Big would trot behind the car all the way home.

Before Big, I'd always had success training dogs. I once owned a cocker spaniel named Pumpkin. She could perform fifteen or twenty tricks, including climbing a ladder and sliding down a slide, sitting up on her hind legs and falling over as if dead when shot with an imaginary gun, and the always-helpful shutting the door and answering the phone. I don't mean she answered the phone by barking into it; that would just be strange. Rather, if I was in another room and heard it ring, I'd shout, "Answer," and seconds later, Pumpkin would arrive with the cordless phone in her mouth. Made for some slobbery conversations, but that was the price of a few saved steps.

I mention Pumpkin so you'll understand my frustration with Big. He wasn't a bad dog, just a difficult one. Instead of answering the phone, he'd sit on it. Instead of climbing a ladder, he'd chew on a ladder-back chair. And unless I was close enough to physically control him, he ignored my commands.

That all changed the day I purchased a training collar. As you may know (or may not want to know), these collars have electrodes that protrude into a dog's neck. When activated by a handheld transmitter, they emit a mild shock, reminding the dog who's really in charge—*the human*. The day it came in the mail, I thought about first testing it on myself, just to be sure it wouldn't injure Big. But then I came to my senses and strapped it around his muscular neck. Not long after, I watched him wander discreetly into the kitchen, stand in front of the refrigerator, and look around to make sure nobody could see him. Then he placed his paws on top of the refrigerator and began fishing for a loaf of bread. Just as he was about to nudge the prize into his salivating mouth, he suddenly, and with an exclamatory yelp, changed his mind.

He never stole a loaf of bread again.

I've occasionally wondered whether life would be easier if I could place a training collar on all the difficult people in my life.

The transformation in Big's behavior was immediate and long-lasting. In a few weeks, I hardly used the shock collar at all. He stayed out of the kitchen and stopped running off when the front door was open. Paul could take him for a walk without being dragged behind him. Even an old dog can learn new tricks when properly motivated.

I've occasionally wondered whether life would be easier if I could place a training collar on all the difficult people in my life. You know, give them a little zap when they misbehave. I'd certainly be less difficult if I wore one.

Of course, I'm only joking. No sane person would willingly wear a training collar or shock another person. But in another sense, isn't that what we do every day? Don't we send verbal and nonverbal zingers intended to change people by putting them in their place or correcting their perceived misdeeds? Unfortunately, those zingers never fix anyone. In fact, they usually make matters worse.

The truth is, there is no push-button fix for the problem people in our lives. I'm not talking about bad people who seek to destroy us or those we love. I'm referring to people who make a bad decision, acknowledge it was a bad decision, and then repeat it.

People like Simon Peter.

I realize I could have used Judas or the Pharisees to illustrate problem people. But Judas was a bad man and the Pharisees were religious hypocrites who hated Jesus. Most of the problem people in our lives aren't out to get us arrested or killed. They're likely well-intentioned people who need to grow in an area or two.

I think if I had known Peter, I would have found him a challenging guy to be around. He was impulsive, disrespectful, and disloyal. He was also bold, insightful, and passionate. Of course, his upside set him apart as a leader and a man of reckless faith. That's why we know so much about him. Besides Jesus, he's mentioned more than any other person in the Gospels. He spoke more than the other disciples and was spoken to by Jesus more than any other. No other disciple reproved Jesus or suffered as many reproofs from the Lord.

Most of the problem people in our lives aren't out to get us arrested or killed. They're likely well-intentioned people who need to grow in an area or two.

Make no mistake about it, Jesus spent time and effort dealing with Peter. And his example shows us how we can interact with the problem people in our lives.

A Thoughtless Interruption

One encounter happened at night on the summit of Mt. Tabor in northern Israel, where Jesus took Peter, James, and John to pray. As they would months later in Gethsemane, Peter and his companions fell asleep. When they awoke, they witnessed Jesus with clothing as bright as lightning. By his side stood Moses and Elijah in "glorious splendor," talking about the Lord's imminent departure (Luke 9:28-32).

The Gospel writer Mark says they were "terrified" (Mark 9:6, ESV). That's a believable description. If I woke to that scene, I'd be very, very quiet, like a sleeping shadow. Not Peter. When he saw Moses and Elijah leaving the mountaintop, he wanted to stop them. "Master," he blurted out, "it is good for us to be here. Let us put up three shelters—one for you, one for Moses and one for Elijah" (Luke 9:32-33). Luke editorializes by adding that Peter didn't know what he was saying.

In the presence of a transfigured Jesus and two of the greatest men in world history, Peter wanted, of all things, to keep them on the mountain by building shelters. No questions about their discussion. No questions about the glory of Jesus' transfigured body. No questions at all. Just a suggestion that he and the other disciples build shelters.

I wonder if Peter expected Jesus to say, "Great idea, Peter. Get to work."

Instead, everyone stood breathlessly still, silently watching as a cloud appeared and a booming voice announced, "This is my Son, whom I have chosen; listen to him" (Luke 9:35).

Peter quickly shelved his construction project.

> *In the presence of a transfigured Jesus and two of the greatest men in world history, Peter wanted to keep them on the mountain by building shelters.*

This story reminds me of an early Steve Martin movie, *The Jerk*. Acting the part of Navin R. Johnson, Martin plays the adopted white son of poor African American sharecroppers who is raised naively oblivious of his adoption, a fact that's as obvious as the color of his skin. He stands out in his family not just for that reason, but also because he has the rhythm of a pet rock.

One day, after his mother finally tells him the truth about his identity, a distraught Navin leaves home to start a new life. He goes from rags to riches and back again. In most situations, he demonstrates a hilarious social ineptitude. When he loses his wealth, he ignores his grieving wife and walks though his mansion saying, "I don't need anything . . . except this, and this, and this," as he picks up a TV remote, an ashtray, a paddle ball, matches, a lamp, a chair, and a magazine. He shuffles out of the house carrying the things he "needs," while his wife sits in the den in tears. Possessing innocence and a lack of malice, Navin R. Johnson wasn't a bad person, just a difficult one.

Like Steve Martin's character, Peter lacked an awareness of the rules of social interaction. He seemed unaware of social cues and at times failed to filter his speech, like he did with his blurted question on the Mount of Transfiguration. In that instance, Jesus allowed his Father to correct the misspoken disciple.

Jesus allowed his Father to correct the misspoken disciple. Sometimes it's best to say nothing and let God deal with difficult people.

Sometimes it's best to say nothing and let God deal with difficult people. Jesus didn't always choose to hold his tongue, though. He rebuked Peter, corrected him, and taught him. In each situation, he engaged him in the appropriate way.

The Betrayal

The most infamous exchange between Peter and Jesus occurred the night before the Lord's crucifixion. As Jesus emotionally shared about his impending betrayal, desertion by his best friends, and brutal death, he looked at Peter and told him, "Simon, Simon, Satan has asked to sift you as wheat. But I have prayed for you, Simon, that your faith may not fail. And when you have turned back, strengthen your brothers."

But Peter replied, "Lord, I am ready to go with you to prison and to death."

Jesus answered, "I tell you, Peter, before the rooster crows today, you will deny three times that you know me" (Luke 22:31-34).

To Peter, such a future seemed impossible—he would *never* betray his Lord. So he challenged the truthfulness of the Lord's words. Later, while Jesus was being held at the home of the high priest, Peter warmed his hands at a nearby fire. There, the fisherman was asked three times if he was a follower of Jesus. And three times he denied any association. Peter's denials didn't go unnoticed. As soon as the last denial left his mouth, a rooster crowed and Jesus turned, looking into Peter's eyes. The cowardly disciple remembered the Lord's prophecy and ran away, weeping bitterly (Luke 22:54-62).

All of Peter's bravado and good intentions washed to sea, and he came face to face with the reality of his weakness and inadequacy. Jesus had seen it all along, but now Peter saw it.

All of Peter's bravado and good intentions washed to sea, and he came face to face with the reality of his weakness and inadequacy.

Peter likely remembered only the Lord's prediction of his failure. He may have forgotten Jesus' promise that, after falling, he would get back up. I'm sure chains of despair wrapped around him, offering no way of escape.

But Jesus didn't forget Peter. After the Lord's crucifixion and burial, an angel appeared to three women at the tomb and told them, "Go, tell his disciples *and* Peter, 'He is going ahead of you into Galilee. There you will see him, just as he told you'" (Mark 16:7, emphasis added). Notice that the angel singled out Peter.

Jesus also appeared to Peter alone in a one-on-one meeting (Luke 24:34). We can only imagine what happened . . . tears, hugs, expressions of sorrow and forgiveness. Later, while sitting on the shore eating fish cooked on an open fire, Jesus asked Peter three times if he loved him. And three times, Peter affirmed his love. With each affirmation, the Lord commanded Peter to care for his sheep (John 21:15-17).

How did Jesus deal with Peter during this time of denial and repentance?

- He spoke the truth in love. When he predicted Peter's impending failure, he also extended hope that Peter would recover and be used by the Lord.
- He prayed for Peter.
- He forgave and reinstated him.

Reckless Faith

Though Peter could be difficult, I find it encouraging that he possessed a bold and reckless faith in Jesus. He had the kind of faith that drove a sane man to leap off a boat in the middle of a storm because he thought he could walk on water.

Peter had the kind of faith that drove a sane man to leap off a boat in the middle of a storm because he thought he could walk on water.

It was nighttime, and Peter and the other disciples were in a boat when an angry storm hit the Sea of Galilee, turning the water into a roaring, rolling, angry monster.

As the exhausted disciples pushed and pulled on the oars, the wind and waves shoved back harder, holding the boat in place. Suddenly, their fatigue morphed into terror. In the distance, they saw what appeared to be a ghost walking on the water. And then they heard a familiar voice.

"Take courage!" he said. "It is I. Don't be afraid" (Matthew 14:27).

Was it Jesus . . . walking on the water?

Above the flapping sail and crashing waves, those were the only words Peter needed to hear. As quickly as he could cup his hands around his mouth, he shouted, "Lord, if it's you . . . tell me to come to you on the water" (Matthew 14:28).

I love to imagine Jesus' face the moment he heard Peter's request. Did he laugh, shaking his head in amazement? Did a grin slowly transform his mouth, or was it a quick, full-faced smile—the kind that makes your eyes squint? After a hard and tiring day, Peter's request had to have been an encouragement. In the midst of the storm, Jesus shouted back a single word, "Come" (Matthew 14:29).

With the wind spitting sea-spray on his face and slapping his robe, Peter, the difficult disciple, didn't hesitate. He stepped from the boat and placed one foot on H_2O. And then the other leg left the boat, both feet now resting on water, his body held up by—what?—the power of God, unleashed by a fisherman's faith. In that moment, Peter performed the ultimate Jesus Experiment, and the Lord proved he could infuse a follower with the miraculous.

The Jesus Experiment

I'm captivated by the image of Jesus walking on water, leaving footprints for us to follow. My faith is revitalized by the realization that, in following his footsteps, I, too, can do what he did.

Every bit as compelling, though, is that Peter, the difficult disciple, left his own footprints on the water. That's something all believers should desire from the deepest part of their souls, for their lives to emulate Christ's life. I know I want to walk on water.

I want to leave liquid footprints that bear testimony to the Lord's supernatural power . . . footprints that encourage others to follow in the steps of Jesus.

It's true that Peter momentarily doubted and began to sink. But he didn't sink far, because he didn't *abandon* his faith. He only took his eyes off Jesus for a moment, as we all do. When he called for help, the Lord grabbed his hand and rescued him. No wonder Jesus endured Peter's shortcomings. He not only saw Peter's failings, he also saw flashes of a fearless faith. He saw someone who, in spite of his weaknesses, had the kind of faith that would unleash the Father's power, changing the world.

> *I want to leave liquid footprints that bear testimony to the Lord's supernatural power . . . footprints that encourage others to follow in the steps of Jesus.*

What did Jesus feel and think?

Immediately before Jesus mentions Peter's impending betrayal and denial, we're told he was "troubled in spirit" (John 13:21). Jesus knew his death would create pain for those he loved. And he knew Peter would deny him. But he was also aware that Peter's failure would create more pain, and this distressed him more.

We also read, "Having loved his own who were in the world, he loved them to the end" (John 13:1, ESV). In the upper room, Jesus felt a strong affection for his closest friends—the kind of affection you'd feel if you knew you would soon die and leave a loved one behind. It's clear Jesus was thinking about Peter's impending failure, sorrow, and forgiveness when he corrected him.

The Lord's response to Peter says we need to manage our emotions when we encounter difficult people so we can give God a chance to deal with them.

What I feel and think

Each time we encounter a difficult person, we need to ask ourselves, *What would Jesus feel and think right now?*

The problem for most of us is knowing whether we should speak or stay silent. Of course, in certain social situations, we would probably say nothing. Later, we might offer a correction that doesn't need to be offered. What Jesus demonstrated with Peter is that it's best for emotions to inform, rather than dictate, a response. Obviously, this can be hard.

I know I find it hard to control my emotions when someone sidetracks me. A few years ago, I was speaking in Anchorage, Alaska, when a man in the back of the church stood and yelled, "I don't believe a word you're saying."

Now, it's not like I was talking about alien abductions or prenatal memories—neither of which I've experienced. I was talking about how God brings change to the world one person at a time. After the initial, three-second shock wore off, I saw the guy sit down. Pretending nothing had happened, I continued with my message. A few minutes later, it happened again—he stood and shouted the same thing: "I don't believe a word you're saying."

The Lord's response to Peter says we need to manage our emotions when we encounter difficult people so we can give God a chance to deal with them.

Granted, I wasn't standing on a mountaintop with my two buddies Moses and Elijah, but I was in the middle of conveying an important point. So I was thankful when two ushers—no, not God—quietly settled the man down. Don't get me wrong, I would have preferred if a cloud had floated into the auditorium through the front door and God's booming voice had broken the awkward silence: "Listen to Bill; he's got something you need to hear."

In that situation, I was fortunate to have ignored the difficult person. It's important to remember, though, that when our style must be more confrontational—which may be called for—we need to make sure we're acting out of love, as Jesus always did.

When our style must be more confrontational, we need to make sure we're acting out of love, as Jesus always did.

Of course, the problem in applying this principle is that Jesus *knew* Peter would fall *and* get back up. We don't have that kind of insight into the difficult people in our lives. I wish we did. Then again, do they need us to know they'll recover from a fall? Or do they simply need us to believe God will use them in the future? God's redemptive power is what we must think about in the face of a difficult person's failure.

What did Jesus say and do?

On the night Peter betrayed Jesus, and in the days following, every word Jesus spoke to Peter was intended to strengthen, restore, and enable him to effectively care for others. Jesus' actions also reflected this purpose. Isn't that why he appeared alone to Peter? Isn't it why he asked Peter three times if he loved him? Isn't it why he told Peter three times to feed, or care for, his sheep?

What I say and do

I recently received an e-mail from a close friend who has struggled with addictive behavior for years. John is one of the most naturally gifted artists I know. His quick sense of humor could soften the heart of a bitter recluse. His social antenna is tuned into the subtle signals of our culture; and when he writes, he captures what he has seen and heard with descriptive words that flow from his fingers with the ease of casual conversation. I love him like a son and would literally give my life if I thought it would save his.

For years I've struggled alongside him. He detoxed in my home only to medicate again when tormented by emotional pain. His most recent fight for freedom took him to another part of the country. He felt he needed to get away from the bad influences in his hometown. I thought he was doing well until I got an e-mail saying he was hooked on Valium again—a drug he had detoxed from five years before and sworn he would never get addicted to again.

Sensing his discouragement, I reminded him of the progress he had made. I told him most addicts who find freedom relapse numerous times before finally breaking free. I assured him all of his disappointments would be used by God to make him a greater man—something I believe for him even when he doesn't believe it for himself.

All of his disappointments would be used by God to make him a greater man.

One day, John will be clean, and he will stay that way. One day, he will bring to reality the dream God has placed in his heart, to provide hope to the hopeless through the artistic passions God has given him. One day his story, like Peter's, will encourage other difficult people and those who love them.

When people we deeply love and care for disappoint us, they become difficult. At that time, we must trust God to speak into their lives and redeem them and the situation. We need to have a perspective that looks forward to their restoration, not backward at past failures or inward at the current pain.

Dealing with difficult people is challenging because, like Peter, they tend to say and do inappropriate and hurtful things. Our challenge is to view them through the eyes of Jesus and treat them as he would. Lord willing, as we follow Jesus onto the water, his miraculous power will enable us to love difficult people as he loved Peter.

Living the Jesus Experiment

This Week

When you encounter difficult people, ask yourself what Jesus would feel, think, say, and do in the same situation. Now take note of your own responses. What are you feeling, thinking, saying, and doing? As you abide in Jesus, pray that God will enable you to treat the difficult people in your life as he would.

Ask

Read Luke 22:31-34; Luke 22:54-62; Luke 24:34; and John 21:1-25. On the chart on page 243, examine the left-hand column, noting what Jesus felt, thought, said, and did when interacting with Peter, a difficult person in his life.

We're told that Jesus loved his disciples and was troubled just before he told Peter about his impending betrayal. How do you think he emotionally and mentally processed those feelings?

_____

_____

_____

_____

What three things did Jesus do in restoring his relationship with Peter? How would following his example help you deal with a difficult person in your life?

_____

_____

_____

_____

_____

Observe

Think of a difficult person in your life. How would you rate him or her on the following characteristics (on a scale from 1 to 10)?

____ Unreliable	____ Fun-loving
____ Impulsive	____ Creative
____ Lazy	____ Unfocused
____ Argumentative	____ Determined
____ Insensitive	____ Visionary
____ Risk taker	____ Doesn't learn from past mistakes

Think of a specific, recent situation when this person caused you a problem. Fill in the center column of the chart (p. 243), recording how you felt, thought, spoke, and acted in this situation when self-reliant.

Evaluate

Fill in the right-hand column of the chart, recording what you believe you would feel, think, say, and do in that same situation if you were abiding in Jesus and followed his example.

Apply

Write specific steps to help you feel, think, speak, and act like Jesus the next time you encounter this person. Spend a few minutes in prayer, asking God to guide you.

_____

_____

_____

_____

_____

Here are a few suggestions to get you started:

- Memorize verses such as James 6:2; Romans 12:18; and 2 Corinthians 5:17.
- Record in your journal how you were able to encourage a difficult person in your life.
- Ask God to give you wisdom to know when you should stay quiet and let him speak to the difficult people in your life.

One Week Later

Record your thoughts about how living the Jesus Experiment over the last week helped you deal with difficult people like Jesus did. How did abiding in Jesus and following his example make your life more abundant?

_____

_____

_____

_____

_____

_____

_____

_____

_____

_____

_____

_____

_____

_____

_____

_____

_____

REGARDING DIFFICULT PEOPLE

What did Jesus . . .	What do I . . .	
Feel? John 13:21 says Jesus was "troubled in spirit." John 13:1 says he "loved his own." While troubled in spirit, Jesus felt a loving affection for Peter.	*Feel when self-reliant?*	*Feel when abiding in Jesus?*
Think? Though we're not told exactly, it appears Jesus thought he needed to warn Peter of his future failure and encourage him with a promise of his prayers and Peter's reinstatement. (Luke 22:31-34)	*Think when self-reliant?*	*Think when abiding in Jesus?*
Say? Jesus warned Peter, assured him he would pray for him, told him he would turn back after falling, and reinstated him with a commission to care for and feed Jesus' sheep. (Luke 22:31-34)	*Say when self-reliant?*	*Say when abiding in Jesus?*
Do? Jesus appeared alone to Peter. (Mark 16:7; Luke 24:34) Jesus looked when Peter denied him. (Luke 22:61) Jesus appeared by the Sea of Galilee, talked and ate with the disciples, and met with Peter. (John 21:1-23)	*Do when self-reliant?*	*Do when abiding in Jesus?*

Download full-size charts and study questions at www.jesusexperiment.com.

Final Thoughts on the Jesus Experiment

SOMETIMES, PROFOUND LESSONS are discovered when we least expect them.

Marketing professional Tom Wood tells about the day he climbed Mt. Fuji, Japan's tallest mountain. To reach the summit by sunrise, he and his friends started the five-hour trek at midnight. Along the way, he saw a ninety-two-year-old woman who, according to her companions, had made the climb more than fifty times and had already spent five days on this attempt.

Curious, he stopped her and asked the secret of her success. Instead of offering Tom a nugget of wisdom, the elderly woman simply said, "Excuse me, I'm climbing the mountain."

Her response seemed rude to Tom, and it annoyed him. He turned away and continued his trek, leaving her behind.

Beside the trail were a series of shacks whose owners sold food and drink to travelers. As Tom and his friends approached the summit, one of the store owners coaxed them into his ramshackle hut, where they sat down and had a few drinks. By the time they returned to the climb, the sun had risen. They hustled to the summit and found more than a thousand people enjoying the view and basking in the morning sun.

As he looked around, Tom spotted the old woman sitting on a rock with her hands on her knees. Only then did he understand and appreciate her answer. She had been *focused* on climbing the mountain and reaching the summit by sunrise. He was on a hike and was easily distracted. She was on a mission.[29]

As we seek to know Jesus and experience the abundant life he offers, we too must remain focused. We must ignore distractions that would prevent us from knowing him better. If we will do this, Jesus will meet us in refreshing ways.

The biggest surprise I've had with the Jesus Experiment is that I see Jesus differently than I used to. Something about considering his feelings and thoughts has forced me to see him as a complete person. It's almost as if he changed from a two-dimensional cardboard cutout to a three-dimensional, real-life person.

I never intended the Jesus Experiment to be a Bible study or even a book to be read, pondered, and then put down. I hope it has provided you with fresh insights into Jesus. I hope it has helped you experience a real-time connection with Jesus so you can discover in a fresh way, every day, the joy and peace he offers.

I'm convinced you will—as you live the Jesus Experiment.

Host a Church-Wide Jesus Experiment

THE JESUS EXPERIMENT will strengthen your church by triggering growth on Sunday morning and in small groups while demonstrating the life of Christ to your community. This exciting experiment will engage the people in your church with a real-time connection with Jesus Christ that will transform their lives and your church.

Find all of the resources you'll need to host the Jesus Experiment by going to **www.jesusexperiment.com.**

Acknowledgments

I'M FORTUNATE SO many insightful people helped me along the way as I wrote *The Jesus Experiment*. And I'm glad I can pull them onto center stage and thank them.

My wife, Cindy, whose jaw is no longer locked, continually challenged me to put what I was learning into practice. Something she's still doing by example and exhortation.

My son Paul invested many, many hours editing the manuscript, not once but three times. His insights were one reason this book was the most difficult I've ever written. He just kept spotting weaknesses and inconsistencies that needed fixing. He didn't shy away from pointing out flaws and urging me not to settle for less than the best I could do. "We need one more edit," he said when I thought we had run out of time. And then Tyndale gave us one more week and so we gave it another look.

I'm thankful to my home church, Rolling Hills Community Church in Tualatin, Oregon, for using some of the chapters for a five-week series. This was early in the process and I finished each chapter just in time to hand it over to the staff team. I'm especially grateful to lead pastor Bill Towns and my longtime friend Dave Carr for all the time they invested in the series.

Tyndale editor Dave Lindstedt did an excellent job focusing the fuzzy places, as well as pointing out a few major chapter changes that needed to be made. I especially liked that he's a night owl like me and late e-mails were always responded to quickly, no matter the time.

Speaking of Tyndale, I want to thank associate publisher Jan Long Harris, who urged me to get to work after seeing my proposal for *The Jesus Experiment*. And I'll always be thankful for John Van Diest, founder and former publisher of Multnomah Press and current finder of talent for Tyndale, who published my first book many years ago and keeps urging me to write. John recently told me he thought the greatest books were yet to be written. Those words express the optimism of his life.

Tyndale designer Stephen Vosloo for the brilliant cover.

Mona Kruger for her friendship and for sharing her story.

The anonymous readers who reviewed the book for Tyndale before the editors got to work. Thanks for your efforts and insights.

The copyeditors, who made sure every period and comma was in place.

Years ago, my friend Dr. Rodney L. Cooper opened a critical door for me into the publishing world. I told him I would never forget and I haven't. Thanks, Rod. Without you, this book would likely be only a dream.

Notes

1. David Needham, *Birthright* (Sisters, OR: Multnomah, 1999), 106–107. I'm thankful to Dr. Needham for his excellent insights on a believer's identity in Christ, as well as the lightbulb illustration.

2. Ibid., 139–140.

3. Malcolm Gladwell, *Outliers* (New York: Little, Brown, 2008), 40–41.

4. Ibid., 52.

5. David Needham, *Birthright*, 136.

6. A. T. Robertson, *Word Pictures in the New Testament*, (New York: R. R. Smith, 1930), 212.

7. Luke 22:44. A medical explanation of Jesus' sweating blood can be found at http://www.apologeticspress.com/articles/2223.

8. The stars depicted in Revelation 12:4 represent angels who followed Lucifer in his fall and were swept from heaven.

9. http://www.yacht-sea.net/mega-yacht-profiles/octopus.html.

10. The *temptation cycle* is a term I devised and explain in detail in my book *When Good Men Are Tempted* (Zondervan, 2007).

11. Fritz Rienecker and Cleon Rogers, *Linguistic Key to the Greek New Testament* (Grand Rapids, MI: Zondervan, 1982), 128.

12. Gloria Pitzer; http://www.iwise.com.

13. Merriam-Webster's Collegiate Dictionary, 11th Edition, © 2006 Merriam-Webster, Incorporated; http://www.merriam-webster.com.

14. William Shakespeare, *Julius Caesar*, act 4, scene 3.

15. George W. Cecil, in *Respectfully Quoted: A Dictionary of Quotations Requested from the Congressional Research Service*, Suzy Platt, ed. (Washington, DC: Library of Congress, 1989).

16. "Too Much Month (At the End of the Money)," written by Bob DiPiero, Dennis Robbins, and John Sherrill.

17. Merriam-Webster's Collegiate Dictionary, 11th Edition, © 2006 Merriam-Webster, Incorporated; http://www.merriam-webster.com.
18. Dart Center for Journalism & Trauma, "Self-Study Unit 3: Photography & Trauma." The Dart Center is a project of the Columbia University Graduate School of Journalism.
19. Sonja Lyubomirsky, *The How of Happiness* (New York: Penguin, 2007), 126–132.
20. Ibid.
21. Adapted from Robert E. Farrell with Bill Perkins, *Give 'em the Pickle!* (Portland, OR: Farrell's Pickle Productions, 1995), 83–88.
22. Some of the thoughts in this section were adapted from one of my earlier books, *Awaken the Leader Within* (Grand Rapids, MI: Zondervan, 2000), 175–189.
23. Gregg Cantelmo, "How Jesus Ministered to Women," http://bible.org/article/how-jesus-ministered-women#P38_12030.
24. Merriam-Webster's Collegiate Dictionary, 11th Edition.
25. John M. Drescher, *Seven Things Children Need* (Scottsdale, PA: Herald, 1976), 77.
26. Ross Campbell, *How to Really Love Your Child* (Wheaton, IL: Victor, 1987), 45.
27. Ibid., 49
28. Harry F. Harlow, Monkey Love Experiments, The Adoption History Project; http://darkwing.uoregon.edu/~adoption/studies/Harl.
29. Tom Wood, viewed September 30, 2010 on YouTube, http://www.youtube.com/watch?v=GWlzFkguRoY. This link is no longer active.

About the Author

BILL PERKINS'S WIT, insight, and penetrating stories have made him a compelling voice in the Christian community. He has authored or collaborated on twenty books, including *When Good Men Are Tempted, Six Battles Every Man Must Win, 6 Rules Every Man Must Break, When Good Men Get Angry,* and *The Jesus Experiment.*

Bill has a passion for helping men discover their strength in God. He is the founder and CEO of Million Mighty Men and served as a senior pastor for twenty-four years. He holds degrees from the University of Texas and Dallas Theological Seminary.

With his talent for humor, candor, and tackling tough issues head-on, Bill is a sought-after speaker for both Christian and corporate groups. He has addressed men's groups across the world and conducted business and leadership seminars across the country for companies such as Alaska Airlines and McDonald's. He has led chapels for major league baseball teams, and appeared on nationally broadcast radio and television shows, including *The O'Reilly Factor*.

Bill and his wife, Cindy, live in West Linn, Oregon. They have three sons and two grandchildren.

For more information on Bill's ministries, and to follow his blog, visit www.billperkins.com.

Online Discussion *guide*

TAKE *your* TYNDALE READING EXPERIENCE *to the* NEXT LEVEL

A FREE discussion guide for this book is available at bookclubhub.net, perfect for sparking conversations in your book group or for digging deeper into the text on your own.

www.bookclubhub.net

You'll also find free discussion guides for other Tyndale books, e-newsletters, e-mail devotionals, virtual book tours, and more!

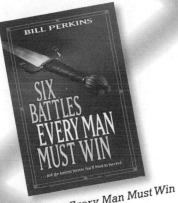